The Best of Prim~~ary Education?~~

To Rita Jean

The Best of Primary Education?
A sociological study of Junior Middle Schools

Ronald A. King

 The Falmer Press

(A member of the Taylor & Francis Group)
London · New York · Philadelphia

UK   The Falmer Press, Falmer House, Barcombe, Lewes, East Sussex, BN8 5DL

USA   The Falmer Press, Taylor & Francis Inc., 242 Cherry Street, Philadelphia, PA 19106–1906

First published 1989

Library of Congress Cataloging-in-Publication Data

King, Ronald, 1934–
    The best of primary education?: a sociological study of junior middle schools/Ronald A. King.
    p. cm.
    Bibliography: p.
    ISBN 1–85000–602–4. ISBN 1–85000–603–2 (pbk.)
    1. Middle Schools—Great Britain—Case studies. 2. Middle Schools—Research—Great Britain. 3. Educational sociology—Great Britain. I. Title.
    LB1623.K525 1989
    373.2′36—dc20   89–11883
                                                CIP

British Library Cataloguing in Publication Data

King, Ronald, 1934–
The best of primary education?: a sociological study of junior middle schools.
1. Great Britain. Schools. Social aspects
I. Title
370.19′0941
ISBN 1–85000–602–4
ISBN 1–85000–603–2 pbk

Typeset in 11/13 Bembo by
Bramley Typesetting Limited, 12 Campbell Court, Bramley, Basingstoke, Hants. RG26 5EG

Printed in Great Britain by Taylor & Francis (Printers) Ltd, Basingstoke.

Contents

Acknowledgements

My main thanks go to the teachers in the two schools who generously allowed me to observe in their classrooms, and to the headteachers who willingly gave me help and cooperation. They not only made possible the research upon which this book is based, but also made it a pleasant and rewarding experience. I have respected their confidences by the customary use of pseudonyms. I doubt that many, if any, of the children who talked to me remember doing so. They too were tolerant with their errant visitor.

1 The Research and Its Contexts

The walls of the room are covered in pieces of paper. There are paintings of abstract patterns and handwritten 'My memories of last year'. The lower panes of the windows are covered too, with printed posters of animals, plants and country life, and others hand-prepared of 'Our Village'. There are cut-out portions of cartons, '10% bigger' and '15% extra free', lists of names, 'We know our tables', piles of books with written names and titles, 'Word Book', 'Creative Writing', 'Science'.

The room contains thirty children aged between ten and eleven. Some are sitting at tables reading books, others write in books labelled 'Mathematics'. Others stand to roll empty cans on pieces of paper laid on tables, making measurements with rulers. A woman moves around the room, pencil in hand, talking to individuals and groups of children. Two girls smile and laugh quietly as they talk to one another over their open books, pens in hand. The woman looks at them. 'Hannah and Lisa, you are not good for one another. Do you know why?' They look down at the table with embarrassed smiles. 'Too much chattering. Now get on with your work before you make me cross.' She looks at their books. 'Where's the date?' Around the room children write the date on the top line of the page in their book.

In the corner sits a man, looking around the room and writing in a notebook from time to time. Neither the children nor the woman look at him. The room is a classroom in a primary school, a junior middle school for children aged eight to twelve. The children are pupils, the woman they call 'our teacher'; she calls them 'my class'. The man is me. This is a descriptive fragment of the doing of the research that is the basis of this book.

Access and Ethnography

I had in mind to research the education of older children in primary

1

schools when I completed that of younger children in infant-first schools (King, 1978). However, the opportunity did not arise until I obtained a period of study leave during the education year 1983–1984. The research was carried out in two schools in Newbridge, a town of nearly 100,000 population.

Greenleigh is a village on the edge of Newbridge but it is now virtually continuous with the town, although local people will call it 'the village'. Most of the houses are detached or semi-detached owner-occupied, with a few council houses. Mr Kirby, the headteacher of Greenleigh Middle School, readily agreed to my visiting the school. Bell (1969) has nicely sketched the dimensions of observational research. Schools are not, in his terms, 'open systems', like street corners or discos with relatively easy access for research purposes, but 'closed systems' requiring 'sponsorship' for entry. Mr Kirby was my sponsor. The research purpose I outlined to him was vague but honest. As a sociologist, I had a general interest in a period of children's education that had not, at the time, been much researched, particularly not of classroom teaching and learning.

The Greenleigh school was opened in 1972. Its design was, in Bennett, Abdreae, Hegarty and Wade's (1980) classification, one of semi-open plan. 'Classrooms without doors' was the way the teachers described it. There were seven classes, two each for the first three years, in doorless rooms arranged in pairs with a shared smaller room between. These were in a L-shape around a wide corridor with furnished bays, a hall, dining room, kitchen and offices. The one fourth year class was in a closed room, originally intended for audio-visual use.

Mr Kirby introduced me to Mrs Mackenzie, one of the two first year teachers, who agreed to my observing in her classroom. I stressed that I was not an expert in junior-age education, and gave my professional assurance to be confidential about anything I saw or heard.

Not knowing what the qualities of junior-age education were, the best way to find out was to use direct observations — what is usually called *ethnography*. This term is sometimes equated with participant observation. Bell (1969) has pointed out that 'participant observation' varies from total participation with no observation, to observation with no participation. My method was close to the latter. Drawing on my infants' schools research experience, I followed this procedure. My first visit was a short one, not more than an hour, in which I tried to avoid eye-contact with the children; eye-contact being used as a prelude to conversation. I made a longer second visit soon after and, with the teacher's permission, took notes. Only one objected, but after I reluctantly agreed to read them through with her, she withdrew her objection and, having read a page or two, wanted to see no more. After a shorter period of observation, I spent at least two whole days with each class.

Sociologists study *social structures.* In my theoretical perspective, social structures are the patterns of relationships between people. As Collins (1975) puts it, 'Structure in so far as it really occurs . . . can be found in the real behaviour of everyday life'. The social structure of a school class is the pattern of the relationships between the teacher and children. Like all social structures, those of classrooms are not static, but are created by the *actions* of the participants. To be in a classroom at the beginning of the day to observe the teacher and the children relating to one another in what became familiar ways, was to see the creation of a social structure; a structure that ceased to exist at playtime, after school or over the weekend (except in the consciousness of the participants and others).

To study the social relationships that constitute social structures, the sociologist must make some kind of relationship with those whose relationships he or she wants to study. The observer-observed relationship is a social structure used to study another structure. Unless it is made covertly, behind a one-way mirror for example, observation always involves some participation. I wanted to observe things that might have happened had I not been there — unknowable of course. Did my observing change what happened? 'Not really', or 'not at all', was the kind of response I got from teachers at the end of a second or third visit.

At Greenleigh, I was able to observe all eight teachers at work, there being two half-timers for a second year class, starting with the first year and proceeding logically to the fourth. Negotiating access became easier as teachers regarded me 'as part of the scenery' and endorsed my acceptability to one another. Mrs Mackenzie told the staffroom, 'He's quite unobtrusive'. One teacher asked me when I was going to visit her. She was planning 'to do some messy art work', which she didn't do very often, and I might miss it. I sometimes felt I was getting a special performance, but rarely so.

The children were well-used to adults other than their teacher being in the classroom from time to time, including student teachers and their tutors, and advisers. They showed little curiosity about me, especially as I did not initially show an active interest in what they were doing. Some tried to make sense of me by asking, 'Are you hoping to be a teacher?'; 'Have you come to make a report on Mrs Smith (their teacher)? We saw you taking notes'. I explained, truthfully, I was just a visitor, interested in what was going on. Sociologists study people and are themselves studied.

It is impossible to make written notes of everything that happens in a classroom, but I tried to record what commonly happened, including sequences of talk. Much 'observation' is listening. With the teachers' co-operation I was able to tape-record some activities. At the end of each day, I would write notes on my notes.

People relating to one another to create social structures are not just behaving but *acting*. That is, they have some subjective purpose or purposes to their behaviour. With experience it is possible to infer what peoples' subjective purposes are from direct observation; we do it all the time in everyday encounters with one another. However, any inferences are better confirmed by the subjects' accounts of their action using *interviews*. Whilst observing I would make an *aide memoire* of questions to put to the teacher at some convenient time, usually at the end of the day. Knowing I had seen and heard things as they happened, teachers often gave their accounts of events without my asking. These were very informal interviews, close to conversations. I made notes of the exchanges as soon as possible afterwards.

I had tried to interview infants (King, 1978, 1984) but they seemed to lack the quality of reflexivity to consider and account for their own actions. However, I found that eight-year-olds could be productively interviewed — being used to having 'discussions' in some of their lessons. I used two methods. Firstly, asking brief questions during the course of classroom activities when the children were used to my presence. This could be done adventitiously when children were working outside the classroom or when someone was not doing games or physical education. Secondly, I taped interviews with groups of three children, usually two from each class chosen by the teacher as being reasonably representative. I had to learn not to lead the children. If I did not let them chatter on, the tape showed I sounded just like a teacher guiding them to an acceptable response.

At the end of my time at Greenleigh, Mr Kirby accepted my suggestion that I gave an account of my work to the staff at an after-school meeting, where, perhaps partly from politeness, they broadly confirmed my interpretation of my observations. Mr Kirby concluded, 'I think you got it (my account) very well right. Sometimes embarrassingly right'.

The second school was St. George's Middle school, a church school, in an older residential area of Newbridge. Whereas Greenleigh had a distinctive catchment area, the children of St. George's came from many parts of the town, but mainly from the area adjacent to the school of older terraced houses, and a nearby estate of mainly semi-detached houses, as well as some children from council houses. Information provided by the headteachers showed the social composition of Greenleigh to be mainly middle-class, with 54 per cent of fathers with non-manual occupations, St. George's social composition was mainly working-class, with 65 per cent of fathers with manual occupations.

The oldest parts of St. George's were Victorian with more recent post-war additions and a temporary classroom. There were two first and two second year classes, three third and three fourth year classes, Mr Gordon, the headteacher, described the ways of the school as 'traditional'. The teachers also used the term, but also 'old fashioned'.

I had told Mr Kirby at Greenleigh that I would be asking Mr Gordon if I could visit his school, and Mr Kirby agreed to act as referee for me. Mr Gordon agreed to my request, although he doubted that all the teachers would allow me to observe their classes, some would object 'on principle'. However, I did observe all ten teachers at work (two were not class teachers) although not in the orderly sequence of first to fourth years as at Greenleigh. I used the same methods of observation and interview as at Greenleigh, although it was difficult to interview children, the school being rather crowded, short of quiet spaces and electric sockets.

I gave an account of my work to the staff at the end of my time there, at a free lunch provided by the headteacher. These meetings were a way of confirming my interpretations, but also, out of politeness to give something back to people who had been helpful and cooperative, in a most altruistic way. Some expressed satisfaction to me privately in having talked about their concerns with someone who was interested and non-judgmental.

Other Methods of Research

Observations and interviews — ethnography — were my main methods, with nearly four hundred hours of classroom observations and nearly a third of a million words of notes. I also observed and informally interviewed outside classrooms in corridors, playgrounds, assemblies, and at events such as Harvest Festival and Prize Day.

This ethnography was supplemented in a number of ways. Schools are full of paper. I read and made notes of the books and worksheets the children used, and of the things they wrote and drew. With the headteachers' permission, I had access to the school records, children's files, reports to parents and governors and the school log.

In addition to this *documentation,* I took advantage of the literacy of the older children, by their completing a simple *questionnaire.* A draft (slightly different in the two schools) was approved by the headteachers and the teachers concerned, and the schedule given to children in the five third year classes. They had all observed me observing them, and I had interviewed some of them. I explained, I hadn't time to talk to them all, but written questions and answers were a reasonable substitute. To emphasize the confidential nature of the exercise, each completed questionnaire (it took about twenty minutes) was sealed by the child in an envelope.

I made a quick, simple analysis of the response in each class, reported these to the headteachers and teachers concerned, who agreed to my letting the children know too. This I did to the whole class, inviting them to comment on the results, the whole exercise being tape recorded. I have always tried to provide some feedback to my research subjects, but this was the first time with pupils (King, 1987). Like most educational researchers I used the prevailing authority relationship to my advantage. The children were not asked their permission to be observed, interviewed or complete the questionnaire. However, I am not greatly worried by the ethics of this. A methodological consideration is whether they orientated their responses to their perceptions of my expectations. I did ask if they felt they had answered as they wanted; they emphatically confirmed.

Throughout the period of the field work, I had many conversations with the two headteachers. At the end of my time in each school, they agreed to be interviewed at length, with tape-recording.

Data Analysis

What I have outlined so far, is the part of research known as *field work,* gathering or perhaps creating data. Creating, since some of it, such as answers to questions, would not have existed without my researching. Indeed, there are no observation notes, without observation.

Analysis follows data generation. A long drawn out process for me, because my study leave was followed by a time of burgeoning administrative duties. Slowly, I analyzed the questionnaires, transcribed the tape-recordings and made content analyses of books and other materials. The core of my data was the classroom observation notes. These were annotated according to the activity observed, such as mathematics or playtime, or typical actions including boy/girl differences, or references to children's age. All the references in each category were then collated. The wholeness of the original classroom events was systematically divided, as in any analysis.

The Contexts of the Research

Research is a social activity, and like all social activities, takes place in particular places and at particular times, as I have outlined. But the time and place of the field work and subsequent analyses, can be put into a number of contexts. Firstly, a more general *research context*.

My approaches to the headteachers were not my first contact with their schools. In 1970, I obtained funding from the Social Science Research Council to research the organization of education in Newbridge, where in 1973 the system of infants' (5–7), junior (7–11) and secondary (11–16 or 18) schools, was changed to first (5–8), middle (8–12), comprehensive (12–16) schools and a tertiary college (16 plus). In the year before reorganization all the schools were surveyed. We, my assistants Joan Fry, Bonnie Lucas and I, interviewed the headteachers and teachers of primary schools about their work and the prospect of reorganization. The results of the survey were sent to each teacher.

I thus had data about Greenleigh and St. George's which could put my recent data into a longer time context. Neither headteacher was in position in 1972, and only six teachers were still working in the same school. None of them remembered the earlier survey. (Why should they?) I was in the interesting position of being able to read the record of what they had said more than a decade earlier and had forgotten and, in some cases actually tell them, to their slight surprise, what they had said.

In 1983, the tenth anniversary of reorganization in Newbridge, I obtained a modest grant from the University of Exeter Research Committee to carry out a postal survey of the eighteen middle schools and middle school departments (in combined 5–12 schools). This was a partial replication of the pre-reorganization survey. I could thus put my detailed study of the two schools in the relative here and now, into the broader contexts of the local system of schools, both in the present and the recent past.

Even broader contexts are *regional, national and historical.* In 1974, the reorganization of local government lead to the Newbridge authority being incorporated into an enlarged Nossex County authority. The reorganization was part of researches at the time, and subsequent changes have been monitored. Nationally, changes have occurred in primary education, similar to those in Nossex and Newbridge. I can explore these through official statistics and such studies as have been made.

The research reported here is part of the general research activities in education, and those in the sociology of education, in particular. Most particularly, it relates to my own, in the infants' and first schools of Newbridge, already referred to (King, 1978). I hope this book will complement the earlier one. I had in mind to research the three middle schools that corresponded to the three infants-first schools of the earlier study. However, two of them had recently appointed headteachers who were reluctant to allow me in at what they saw to be a delicate time for them, and the third was about to retire. Hence, my grateful acceptance of the help of Messrs Kirby and Gordon, and their colleagues.

The *sociology of education* in Britain is not a unified field of study. Since the 1970s when earlier work was largely discredited as 'orthodox' and theoretically functionalist by the protagonists of the 'new' sociology of education, the 'new' has factionalized into varieties of symbolic interactionism and neo-Marxism. My own response has been to continue developing a fairly eclectic neo-Weberian approach (King, 1980, 1985).

Sociologists of education have a problem in writing accounts of their work. Who are they writing for? Are they writing for their fellow academics or professional educators including teachers and students? Academic careers are served by meeting the expectations of the former by showing knowledge and understanding of the relevant literature of theory, other studies and methodological considerations. However, most researchers want their work to be as widely known as possible. Hence, my writing here is more directed towards a non-sociological readership. We sociologists of education should be able to make sense to a body of interested, educated practitioners. Consequently, I prefer to introduce the concepts and theoretical perspectives I have used mainly in my reporting of the research and in the final discussion (chapter 10), rather than in grand preliminary statements.

This kind of presentation has already been made in describing the research. 'Theory' is (or should be) the explanation made of empirical reality. But how that empirical reality is realized is in itself a theoretical act. Our explanations cannot be separated from our methods of obtaining that which we try to explain. As I have written earlier in this chapter, in my theoretical perspective, sociologists study social structures, the patterns of relationships between people; 'schools' and 'classrooms'. In Weber's (1964) perspective, structures are created by the *social actions* of people.

> Action is social so far as, by virtue of the subjective meaning attached to it by the acting individual (or individuals), it takes account of the behaviour of others and is thereby orientated in its course.

In this research children and teachers' behaviour, in relating to one another to create structures, was observed. Their subjective meanings in doing so were obtained through interviews. This process of understanding Weber (1968) called *Verstehen.* This requires in Leat's (1972) words, 'that the sociologists go through a process of re-socialization into his subjects' social world, that is their commonsense constructs and experience'. In a sense, I became a teacher and a child at school.

It is not possible to study social structure as wholes, but only through the behaviour of the individuals who relate to one another to create the structures; what Popper (1957) calls 'methodological individualism'. Although individual teachers and children were observed and interviewed, it was not my purpose or, in my view, that of sociologists in general, to explain why individuals *per se* behaved or acted as they did. Individuals were studied to discover their typical actions as teachers and as pupils in particular situations. This is the discovery of *social types.* Every reported example of behaviour and talk was that of an individual teacher or child, but was typical of others in the same situation. Although individuals are named (through pseudonyms) these names are not socially significant, they are a reminder of the human basis of the analysis.

Ethnography, as used in the anthropological tradition, implies studying a whole way of life. My interest in the adults was as teachers, the children as pupils. This was part of the process Devons and Gluckman (1964) call 'delimiting the field'. 'Within a field thus delimited and isolated the social scientist assumes that there is a system of interrelations which can be considered to be separate from the rest of society'. My 'fields' were two schools. The teachers and children did exist in other 'fields' as husbands, wives, parents, sons, daughters, brothers and sisters, and did interact to create other social structures, families and friendship groups. These could have consequences for that of 'the school', but not necessarily. For example, those teachers who were parents felt this experience was a help in their teaching, but other than their making occasional references to their own children, they were not conspicuously different to other non-parent colleagues in their pedagogy. Most teachers were women, but they were not conspicuously different as teachers compared with their male colleagues. No social significance should be attached to the sex and marital status of the pseudonyms of teachers used here.

Sociological theory, is or should be, attempts to explain what has been shown empirically to happen and, as Ford (1975) puts it, 'Explaining is generalizing. Generalizing is theorizing'. I generalize and theorize about teachers and children as social types. The *comparative process* was used to make generalizations; what was commonly seen and heard. What was particular about junior school teachers and children was established by comparison with those of infants' schools (King, 1978). The teachers and children in the two schools studied were compared to establish was what particular to each. The differences among teachers showed different social types (chapter 7). Comparisons between the children showed social difference between boys and girls, older and younger.

When asked why he wanted to climb Everest, George Mallory is reported to have said 'because it is there'. Educational research is sometimes explained and justified in terms of its usefulness in 'improving' education. When I have been asked why I do my research, I have replied, 'I study a school or classroom "because it is there"'. My search is for understanding of the complex social processes of teaching and learning. It is not my purpose to judge people or practices, that would militate any understanding. Junior middle schools, such as those studied here, were advocated in the Plowden Report (1967), whose committee hoped they would employ, 'the best of primary education'. This is the rhetorical question of my title. I hope that those who have the confidence to make that kind of judgment will be better informed by this book.

2   The Ideology of Junior Teaching

The existence of primary schools called junior or middle schools suggests they are different to those called infants' or first schools. I knew some opinions on the nature of their differences before I started my observations of the former. In my earlier research (King, 1978), some infants'-first school teachers regarded the children's move to the junior middle school as the end of real education. 'We have done our best by these children. Let them (the middle school teachers) do their worst'. The junior-trained headteacher of a combined school, said of his own infants' department, 'It's all play down there. It's mainly getting them used to school. All the learning takes place in the juniors'. The headteachers of infants'-first schools all confessed to a strain in their relationships with the headteachers of their associated junior middle schools, feeling that their methods were misunderstood and unappreciated. Within minutes of my being in Mrs Mackenzie's class at Greenleigh junior middle school, I saw and heard things that would have been rare in an infants'-first school. Junior classrooms are different social worlds to those of infants' (and others). One of the purposes of my study was to describe, analyze and try to explain the nature of the differences.

Most of the things that happen in classrooms are arranged or allowed to happen by the teacher. Just as infants' teachers' actions are related to a set of ideas they hold about the nature of young children and the nature of the learning process, so junior teachers hold a different set of ideas, or *ideology*, about the nature of older children and their learning. Both ideologies are *child-centred*, but with different definitions of 'the child' and learning. I initially inferred the nature of the ideology of junior school teachers from the pattern of their classroom relationships, the social structure of the classroom, which was predicated on the ideology. My interpretation was partly confirmed by individual teachers and by each school staff collectively, with an 'of course' kind of reaction, since it represented their truth, what was real for them.

The education of children moving from infants' to juniors, undergoes an *ideological shift*. Their teachers no longer regard play as learning and 'work' is given primacy. Although the children are manifestly still developing, fourth years are almost all bigger than first years, the extent of the development of their capacity to learn is regarded as fairly finite and variable. Children are defined as varying in their ability, and individual differences are mainly accounted for in these terms. Juniors do behave in ways defined by their teachers as naughty, but unlike infants' teachers, theirs do regard them as being usually knowlingly and intentionally naughty — no longer innocent in this sense. The marks of the ideology of junior school teaching are: the primacy of work, the differentiation and finitization of the ability to learn, and the ascription of children's responsibility for their own behaviour — the end of innocence.

The End of Play-as-Learning and the Primacy of 'Work'

The principle of the primacy of work and the end of play was made clear by Mrs Mackenzie to her first year class in their first few days, as this transcript of my observation notes shows.

> A boy has plastic counters to help with his mathematics. Mrs Mackenzie publicly reproves him. 'I'm watching you laddie. I didn't give you cubes to play with. You're here to work. Do you want to go back to the little school (first school) to play?'.

When I asked the new first years about the things they did in the first school that they no longer did now, they had taken their teacher's definition.

> We played with lego and things, but we're not allowed to play here. It's all work here.

> No play at all?

> Not in the actual school, but you can outside (in the playground).

The end of play-as-learning made play the province of children in the controlled time and space of the breaks between 'work'. For both teachers and children, behaviour that hindered work was 'playing about'.

Infants' teachers believe that children learn best when they are happy doing so. Happiness whilst working in the juniors was a bonus, not a desirable prerequisite of good learning. An item on the third year questionnaire asked if they 'usually enjoyed school'. The majority of children agreed in each class of Greenleigh and St. George's. In the follow-up-class 'discussions' with me, they made it clear that 'school' could mean a number of things in the context of their replies, including 'work' and play time. Several spoke of the boredom of the weekend and holidays.

Their teachers preferred to define when an activity was for enjoyment, as when Mr Smith in discussing their Christmas Play told his class, 'It's a fun thing we want — not a serious thing'. Children could laugh when their teacher joked. 'Timothy, is it possible for you to stop babbling like a brook?' But other classroom laughter would usually be regarded as getting in the way of work. 'Save it till playtime'.

Teachers and children both regarded school work as important, and the latter had learnt this from the former, but from who else? The first years reported that their first school teachers said little about the prospect of the middle school, confirming my own experience. However, their parents had told them that they would have to do more 'work' as had friends and kin already in the middle school. Mrs Mackenzie displayed selected pieces of 'good work' in the corridor outside the doorless classroom to 'impress parents, that it's work here, not play'. They seem to have understood.

All the children interviewed were quite clear as to why school work was important — it was related to paid work in adulthood.

> I think that all the work that you do in school helps you in the work that grown ups are doing now.

> When you are older you get a job better.

Cullingford (1986) had similar responses from the children he interviewed. 'For those (pupils) at primary school, the purpose of education is quite clear. Children are at school to enable them to get jobs'.

Even first year children in my research had an idea of the kind of job they might eventually have. In the third year, the majority of children were able to answer one or both of the questions, 'What job would you *like to do* when you are grown up?' and 'What job *do you expect* to do when you are grown up?', sometimes giving the same answer to both questions. The responses to the former were sometimes almost admitted to be fantasies ('I know it's silly, but I'd like to be a Page 3 girl'), but their teachers were surprised at their thinking about their future occupations very much at all. (Their thoughts were not first stimulated by my asking questions; they talked of jobs in interview without my referring to them.)

Where had they got their ideas from? They reported, and my observations in classrooms confirmed, not from their teachers. Cullingford (1985) had a similar response. 'The (primary) teachers interviewed never mentioned jobs as an aim of education'. The children of Greenleigh and St. George's reported getting ideas from their reading and television but mainly from their parents and other relatives.

> I want to be a carpenter like my dad. He can get me into the firm.

Again, Cullingford's (1985) interviews broadly confirm this. 'All the (primary school) parents saw the purpose of education as that of giving their children the means to gain a living'. My own experience of children, showed that parents and kin were the source of their knowledge of the importance of certification as the link between school and paid work, as with this eight-year-old teachers' daughter.

> If you want to be a teacher or something you have to be able to write and things; and be able to do maths, and really to be able to work to qualify to be a teacher. Certificates, that's what you need.

Some children knew about the examination system.

> My older brother, he's at university. He's taken, he's got, it's twelve O-levels and three A-levels, and you have to pass two A-levels and I think it's seven O-levels and I think I want to get some O-levels. If you can get maths and English O-levels you stand a very good chance of getting a job.'

Teachers' child-centredness placed the value of school-work for children in the here and now. The children and their parents valued it for the adults the children would become. The importance of school-work was taken for granted by teachers, children and their parents. This is an institutionalized ideological element, whose history goes back at least to *elementary education* following the 1870 Act. The schools created by that Act were the precursors of the primary schools created by the 1944 Act, including Greenleigh and St. George's. A few teachers in Newbridge had taught in elementary schools and some must have been pupils, but in the junior middle schools they were all the inheritors and perpetuators of the tradition of the primacy of work, even if what was defined as work had changed and was changing.

Ability Differentiation

It is almost always assumed that children will learn to different degrees what they are taught over a period of time. The explanation of these learning differences varies in time and place. In the nineteenth century, British children's relative 'success' or 'failure' was explained in terms of their hard work or laziness, moral judgments that were used to justify their being corporally punished for poor work. In modern Britain, the common assumption is that children vary in their 'ability' to do school work, and that this can be measured by intelligence tests and standardized attainment tests.

In the nineteenth century, 'intelligence' meant useful knowledge (as in army intelligence still) and no one had an intelligence quotient. Intelligence is a *social construct* (Squibb, 1973), of a particular time and place. Teachers in African primary schools attribute children's learning success to hard work and not to differences in individual ability or intelligence; in this respect 'it is considered a virtue to treat all children alike' (Blakemore and Cooksey, 1981). In the Soviet Union, intelligence tests are dismissed as 'bourgeois pseudo-science' (Grant, 1979).

Infants' teachers do talk of children's 'ability', usually with reference to their reading, but they do not regard ability as being a fixed attribute (King, 1978). For them, individual differences in young children's development meant they could 'spurt' or 'slow' in their capacity to learn. The teachers of juniors broadly accept what Esland (1971) calls the 'psychometric paradigm'; that children's capacity to learn is relatively fixed and broadly estimable. Davis (1943) pointed out, in one of the first sociological considerations of the subject, it is the image of intelligence as a substance that children have different amounts of. This construct of intelligence is institutionalized throughout most of British education. It was officially endorsed for what was to become primary education, by the Hadow Report (1931), drawing upon the work of educational psychologists, including Cyril Burt. The eleven-plus examination and a divided system of secondary education, were predicated upon the construct.

The general acceptance of what Demaine (1979) calls 'IQism' by the teachers of Greenleigh and St. George's is wholly understandable. The local authority record card required regular verbal reasoning and reading-age tests. The fourth year took a verbal reasoning test as part of the allocation procedure for the comprehensive schools.

The headteachers took responsibility for the management of testing, an indication of the importance of both. The teachers, who gave the tests and calculated the results at Greenleigh (the headteacher did so at St.

George's), knew the scores of the children they taught fairly accurately, as shown in this interview.

> *RK:* Do you have any of these IQ measurements in mind when you are thinking how well the children are doing?
> *T:* Yes, I am inclined to, well Rachel has an average IQ.
> *RK:* That's the way you've got it in your head as an average. Could you put a number on it?
> *T:* Yes, I think I can, actually it's about 93 or 94, something like that, you know, lower average.

They used their knowledge of the scores as 'a kind of yardstick of capacity'. Knowledge of the scores was restricted to teachers at St. George's. Parents were not told, because 'They wouldn't understand', although reading ages were sometimes mentioned in reports. Mr Kirby at Greenleigh sometimes used its open plan architecture as a metaphor for his educational thinking, and 'opened' the test scores to the parents. It started when he sent copies of the record card home to parents instead of a School Report, but blanked out the results of the standardized tests. 'But I always felt that the kind of record we keep should be open', and so the next year the results were left unblanked, and 'the reaction of parents was that 98 per cent of them felt they were very pleased to have the actual record and they came and discussed it'. However, in neither school were the children told the scores, at least directly.

Mr Kirby at Greenleigh was concerned that the children might find out from their parents.

> I was anxious that children might get hold of it, and started to compare notes, that they'd got 85 for their verbal reasoning. I don't think for one minute that they would have had any idea what they may have meant.

However, children in both schools knew something unusual was going on when they were tested.

> Mr Kirby has decided it would be useful to give the first years a non-verbal test (NFER Test 28, 1970). The children carry their chairs and tables into the hall. Mrs Mackenzie introduces the exercise as 'some puzzles'. 'This is like a game of riddles'. The children follow her oral instructions.

Mrs Mackenzie worked out the scores for the next day; she expected and got 'a few surprises'. On this occasion, the children did not ask about the exercise, but teachers reported they sometimes did. 'You just flannel a bit. Just tell them its something they don't need to know. They can't do anything about it anyway'.

Although the children did not have direct access to any scores, they did hold a quantitative construct of ability similar to their teachers', describing themselves and others as 'clever', 'brainy', 'bright', 'average' and 'slow'.

Even before the abolition of the eleven-plus, most of the junior schools of Newbridge had, what were called in 1972, 'unstreamed', 'non-streamed' or even 'destreamed' classes. The most recent nomenclature is 'mixed ability' and the headteachers used standardized test scores to mix children. At St. George's, the third year was streamed. This was unusual in the junior middle schools of Newbridge, nationally (Lunn, 1982), and even for 'traditional' St. George's. The headteacher, Mr Gordon, expressed the view, 'There's no right answer, streaming or not streaming, I don't regret streaming them this year'.

His decision was based upon an examination of the verbal reasoning scores and the rooms available. Looking at the distribution graph he felt that he could divide the year group into three classes, each with a fairly-well defined and limited ability-range. They were not known as A, B, and C, but by their class teachers' names. However, the children had a range of terms; 'bright, average and slow'; 'good, not so good and others'; 'top, middle and bottom'.

Unlike their teachers, children made a connection between school work and paid work. Unlike their teachers, they also related 'ability' to do school work to paid work. I asked the children of the third year top stream at St. George's to comment on one of the results of the questionnaire survey

> *RK:* All but two of the jobs (you would like or expect to have) were the sort of jobs where people would say you have to use your brains rather than your hands. Sitting down, reading, writing, with positions of responsibility. Does that surprise you?
>
> *Boy:* Where you move around and do things on your own.
>
> *Another Boy:* They are better jobs.
>
> RK: Would it surprise you if I told you that in Mrs Stephens' class (the middle stream) the proportion of children choosing jobs using their hands, manual jobs, was actually higher than here. Only two in here. Does that surprise you?

> *Children:* No. No.
>   *RK:* Why?
>   *Girl:* Because we're more intelligent.
>   *RK:* OK so what's the connection then?
>   *Girl:* The more, brainy you are the better job you can get.
>   *Boy:* If you're brainy you've got a choice.

Their teacher, who was present, seemed a little discomforted by this dialogue, some of the children being quite elated. I did not want to upset anyone unnecessarily, so I did not put the point to the children in the other classes.

The End of Innocence

In my previous research, a few infants' teachers were defined by their headteachers as not being 'proper infants' teachers' (King, 1978). They did do things differently to their colleagues, and they were aware of their being different. They and the headteachers attributed this to their not being 'infant trained'. They were junior trained. 'Proper infants' teachers' typically used oblique methods of controlling children's behaviour; 'Someone's being silly'. Although young children's behaviour could be defined as naughty by infants' teachers, they were not held to be responsible for their naughtiness; innocent in intent, and not to be directly reproved. The junior–trained infants' teachers used more direct methods of control, 'Don't do that', as did the teachers of Greenleigh and St. George's.

Unlike most infants' teachers, those of juniors *do* hold the children they teach responsible for their own behaviour. They could be badly behaved, in the teachers' definition; they knew they were behaving badly and may have chosen to do so. The responsibility for naughtiness was sometimes clearly attributed.

Scott, you are being deliberately silly. Don't put on that innocent look. I know what you are doing.

The innocent state of infants' was protected from what were defined as unpleasant or upsetting aspects of the outside world by their teachers. The teachers of juniors introduced them to the problems of famine and pestilence, world conflicts (the Iran-Iraq war), and the consequences of natural and other disasters, through television and radio schools' broadcasts, and in discussion of projects and in aid collections. The children did not directly encounter these events (at least not at school) but they were made aware of them.

The different elements of the ideology of junior teaching are not new. In the inter-war years, what Vaughan and Archer (1971) call an *assertive ideology* was used to introduce the new construct of ability. This and the other ideological elements, have *legitimacy* in junior practice. For junior school teachers they have the status of the unexceptional truth. In Schutz's (1972) terms, a *recipe ideology*, accepted ways of doing things. Teachers define children and their learning in accord with their ideology, and they and the children act in ways that tend to confirm the 'truth' of the ideological postulate. To slightly paraphrase Thomas (1926), 'If people (men) define situations as real, they are real in their consequences'. In the descriptions and analyses of the different situations or structures of junior-middle education that follow, teachers' definitions that accord with their ideology will be shown to have real consequences for the children and the teachers themselves.

3 School Work: Mathematics and English

Children and their teachers agreed they were in the juniors to work. Their work was the curriculum, which consisted of subjects, sometimes clearly defined, with different degrees of importance to teachers and taught. They gave most importance to what the teachers sometimes called the 'basics', mathematics and English, the 3 Rs of the elementary school tradition. The national sample of junior school teachers in Barker Lunn's (1984) study, reported activities under these headings being followed more frequently than any others.

Mathematics

Third year children were asked to name the most important thing they did in school. In the mixed–ability classes of Greenleigh and the streams of St. George's, mathematics was named most often. I asked why it was so important. Mathematics, as a kind of school work, was linked to paid work.

> Say you wanted to be a shopkeeper, you'd have to count out money and weigh things. If you are good at maths you can get a better job when you are older.

This connection was not made by teachers, who only occasionally made references to adult uses of mathematics, as when estimating the time of a car journey. Nor was it part of the justification for mathematics in the material used in its teaching and learning.

Mr Kirby had introduced the Fletcher Scheme soon after his appointment as headteacher of Greenleigh, his newly appointed deputy head being a 'very keen Fletcher person'. The national survey of Bassey (1978) showed the scheme to be in common use in junior schools. At

St. George's, teachers used a variety of materials, including *Making Sure of Maths* (Watson and Quinn, 1969), *Four Rules of Number* (Hesse, 1966), *The Schools' Mathematics Project*, as well as their own work cards, but not Fletcher. The adult uses of mathematics they referred to were mainly domestic, shopping and do-it-yourself, like measuring for carpets or putting up wall-tiles.

Although teachers did not attribute the importance of mathematics to its occupational value, they nevertheless made its importance very clear. At St. George's, every child did mathematics every day of the week, at Greenleigh four days of five in the week. Mathematics was the subject always timetabled, always in the morning. 'The best time really, at their most awake', was a common explanation. All the children at St. George's did mathematics homework, and when homework was set at Greenleigh, it was most often mathematics. It was clearly more important than other subjects. A child who had been absent could miss other studies to 'catch-up' with mathematics. Children were seldom sent from mathematics classes for misbehaviour as they were from physical education, drama, music or games.

Teachers regarded children's capacity to do mathematics to vary. Some spoke of 'mathematical ability', and the (occasional) use of non-verbal intelligence tests was thought to be some indicator of this quality. Although mixed-ability classes were the common basis for teaching and learning in the two schools, ability grouping was used for mathematics. At St. George's, a small number of first year children attended a remedial class each morning for mathematics (and language work). The second and fourth years were setted, the third year being streamed. The term 'set' was not used at Greenleigh, but children were taught mathematics in ability groups known by their teachers' names. As the survey of Barker Lunn (1984) showed, mathematics setting is a common practice nationally, as it was in Newbridge. The children were well-aware of the meaning of set membership; the different sets being for the 'quick', the 'slow' ones, the 'good' and those 'who need more help'. The sets were created each year using the results of tests, and once assigned, there was little mobility between groups.

In the sets and streams of St. George's the teachers used whole-class teaching as their basic methods, indeed, this was seen as a benefit of these groupings. Barker Lunn's (1982) survey showed this method was used in a third of junior schools of the size of the two in this research, most commonly with setted or streamed groups. The groups or sets at Greenleigh were further divided, as advised by the authors of the Fletcher Scheme, in 'groups of like ability'. For the teachers it was to 'stretch them' and 'give them the attention they need'. Just as the sets were known by the teacher's name, so the teacher called these groups (commonly three) by the name of one of its members. The children were well-aware of their status, knowing which section of which book each group was on, and calling them, 'top', 'middle' and 'bottom'.

Teachers spent more time controlling the pace of mathematics than any others, generally to increase it.

> I'm sorry my lad, but you'll have to work quicker than this. Only two sums!

With whole-class teaching, the children started their work together, but even when setted or streamed for 'ability', completed different amounts of work acceptable to their teachers by the end of the lesson. At St. George's mathematics homework could be to complete the work set in the lesson, or more exercises of the same kind. The children's attainment was differentiated by how many correct answers they completed in a given time. Mathematics was the only work marked numerically by some teachers.

The pacing of the groups within sets at Greenleigh was more complex than that of the whole classes of St. George's. The Fletcher authors cautioned against 'rush tactics' (Howell *et al*, 1980) since 'mathematical development cannot be hurried, but the "clever" ones must not be held back because of delay on the part of "slow learners"'. However, the general tone of the Fletcher children's material was like that used by teachers most of the time.

> How many (exercises) can you do in 5 minutes? How quick are you? Time yourself.

At Greenleigh, the groups within sets and the sets themselves were quite constant in composition throughout the year, after a few changes in the first few weeks. Having defined the groups as having different mathematical abilities, the teachers paced the individual children's progress to keep the group compositions constant ('because if you're not careful you end up with twenty-seven groups of one'), so confirming the definition of the ability of each group. The definition of the situation had real consequences.

Having introduced new work to each group, the teacher would check each child's progress during the lesson, moving around the groups in the classrooms. If one or two children had a problem the whole group would be taken through the exercise. Children finishing their work before the end of the lesson took it to the teacher's desk where it could be marked as they looked on, or left. Towards the end of the lesson, she would ask all the children who had not left their work or had it marked to bring what they had done to her. Wrong work was to be corrected and missing work completed either in the rest of the lesson, at break time, dinner time or at home, so to be ready to start with the group next time. Some who were 'well behind' could be stopped doing physical education or something else less important, to catch up. Some teachers paced the children's work over longer time units of a week, with Friday as the day of reckoning.

Although the general emphasis was for the child to 'get on', some would be slowed down to keep the group together. Some were deterred from taking work home, if this would take them ahead of others. Learning was teacher-mediated.

Don't go racing ahead Sarah, otherwise you won't know what you are doing.

The children of both schools thought mathematics was the most important thing they did at school. They were asked what they most enjoyed at school. For the third years at Greenleigh it was most often mathematics. Enjoyment was expressed independently of the children's set or group status, which section of which book they were on. They found it difficult to explain why they liked it, but several said it was to do with 'getting it right'. The Fletcher Scheme was managed so that eventually each child did get each exercise right. At St. George's, children varied in how much mathematics they got right in a given time. At Greenleigh, they varied in how long they took to get it right.

In both schools, children knew how well they were doing in relation to one another, but with the Fletcher scheme they could see their likely progress.

I've looked ahead in the Fletcher and I can do some of it, so I expect I could do it.

At Greenleigh, children met their own mathematics targets. At St. George's, mathematics as an open competition created success and failures. One of the homeworks commonly set was to prepare for a Tables Test, with the results made public.

Who got ten out of ten? None? Eight? Seven? Oh dear. Six or less? Sharon! Better write out those tables again.

The competition for success in mathematics at St. George's, could be between groups. One teacher arranged children in their House groups, choosing a child from one group to be the 'champion' to ask a question, 'six-sixes?', to be answered by the teacher-chosen 'challenger' of another group. If correct, this child became the new champion and gained a star for his or her House. If not play as learning, this was fun in learning, with much football-style cheering and encouragement. Success went to the groups, but failure was the individual challenger's or toppled champion's, who acted out their despair, smacking foreheads and miming shooting themselves in the head.

The work of mathematics was presented by the children in written form and orally. The form of presentation of the former was sometimes as important as the correct answer.

That's all squashed. One (number) in each column.

Children were asked to speak their mathematics.

Someone talk me through that subtraction.

And sometimes children found it difficult.

You are silly. As soon as you get someone near you, you shut up like a clam. You *can* do it. Say it.

The Fletcher Scheme recognized this possibility 'You must not allow the children's mathematical progress to be held up by lack of ability to verbalize' (Fletcher 1971, p. 3).

As with infants' teachers (King, 1978), those of juniors recognized that children could do Fletcher's mathematics (to the teachers' satisfaction) without necessarily being able to read the text.

If they have the mathematical ability they can work it out from the diagrams, with a bit of help.

A boy did not know the word 'statistics' when I asked him, but he had done the exercises marked as correct from the book section, titled with the word (Book Three 2 p. 9), but not explained in the text, and had recorded his progress on his mathematics record card at the section marked 'statistics'. Only in mathematics, were children presented with language they were not required to understand.

Schutz (1967), the social phenomenologist whose work influenced the new sociology of education in the early seventies, took the view that what was most 'real' to people, their 'paramount reality', was that of everyday life. The subjects of the curriculum may be regarded as a set of what he called *multiple realities,* distanced from everyday life.

A painting by Rene Magritte shows a pipe and the words 'Ce lui ci n'est pas un pipe' (This is not a pipe). The everyday world objects that occur in mathematics, have the appearance of reality, not the substance.

As part of a lesson on fractions the teacher has written on the board, 'Here is a cake'. There is no cake or even a picture of a cake.

'Right you take that along to the shops and spend twenty four (pence) out of fifty two'. There is no money or shop, and nothing is bought.

The Fletcher authors claim that the scheme deals with 'people and life' (Howell *et al*, 1980), but the reality of everyday life is consistently distanced to create the reality of mathematics.

'Computers' was not a subject of the curriculum in any junior middle school of Newbridge, but both Greenleigh and St. George's had them and they were often talked about in relation to mathematics. Children often mentioned them when talking about the prospect of paid work, 'The future's all computers', and saw a knowledge of them as a help in getting a job. Some had their own at home; in their teachers' opinion for playing games.

The government, through the Department of Education and Science and the local education authorities, encouraged the use of computers in schools by subsidizing their purchase. That of St. George's had been acquired through this scheme, as had one of the three at Greenleigh, where the initiative had been taken by a former deputy headteacher. Although children spoke of them enthusiastically, teachers' views were mixed. In both schools, there was an enthusiast who was attending a course with 'hands on' experience, and quietly proselytized among their colleagues.

It's not just a band wagon. You can't ignore them, they're here.

Mr Kirby, the headteacher at Greenleigh, was more enthusiastic than Mr Gordon at St. George's. He saw them as a tool which he hoped all teachers would use. Mr Gordon was 'not unduly impressed' with something that 'would never take the place of a good teacher'. Some teachers confessed to being frightened by them, a few having dropped out from appreciation courses, 'completely lost', 'will never really understand it'.

The reticence of some teachers probably explains why, in spite of their enthusiasm, only a minority of children used computers, most commonly in small groups for remedial mathematics and on infrequent occasions. At Greenleigh a few enthusiasts used them out of lesson time and a computer club was run at St. George's. If the future is all computers, it was arriving slowly.

English

Third year children named English as the most important thing they did in school only slightly less often than they did mathematics. No other curriculum activity was named as often as these two. English, like mathematics was important to them for its vocational value.

> You learn English cos say you got a secretary job you could write a lot of gibberish if you don't know it properly.

> Well, if you don't pass your English exam (at secondary school) you can't get a job.

No teacher referred to the occupational importance of English, but its general importance was clearly stressed. Activities under its heading were followed everyday of the week and, as with mathematics, in the freshness of the morning at St. George's where homework was set regularly.

English, or as it was sometimes called by teachers, language work, was taught in mixed ability groups at Greenleigh. At St. George's a small group of first year children attended a remedial class each morning for English (and mathematics). The second and fourth years were setted (the third streamed). Children were initially allocated to sets on the basis of their reading ages, verbal reasoning scores and teachers' recommendation. In Barker Lunn's national survey (1982) and in my own of Newbridge, setting of English was slightly less frequent than for mathematics. At St. George's membership of the three English sets and three mathematics sets, was similar in both years; 70 and 74 per cent (second and fourth years). No child was in a first and third set for the two subjects. Commenting on his decision to stream the third year, Mr Gordon said they would have been virtually streamed much of the time together in mathematics and English sets. Teachers saw setting as having advantages for all children. They could 'take the better ones on further', whilst 'the poorer ones' did not get discouraged by seeing others as better.

The range of activities that constituted English or language work was wide; hand-writing, reading, spelling, exercises, discussions, 'creative' writing and drama. Not, in Schutz's (1967) terms a single province of meaning, but a set of multiple realities within itself, and the children learnt what to do in each.

Teachers demonstrated their mathematical competence in teaching it, and so were models for the children. Not all activities of English were demonstrated by teachers. One was *handwriting*, taught in the first two years. The children's task was to copy onto lined paper exactly what the teacher had written on the board or on prepared cards.

> I told you, if I go to a new line you go to a new line.

What she had written was unimportant. Unlike everything else she wrote on the board, they did not need to show they could read or understand it. Sometimes it was not even read aloud to them. The language of handwriting could be meaningless. The exercise was thought to be particularly valuable for 'the less able', 'gives them something to be good at, to be proud of'.

Reading was the most important 'work' of children in infants' — first schools (King, 1978) and was important among the activities of English in the junior middle schools. Children read as 'reading' every day, mainly as an individualized activity from a particular book to themselves or to their teacher. At Greenleigh they followed the Ginn Reading Programme, *Reading 360* (1978). Mr Kirby, the headteacher, had introduced it for the diversity of its material, including the illustrations. He heard every child read during the course of the year, looking for discrepancies between their reading ages, verbal reasoning scores and their current book in the series, urging teachers to 'stretch' any child whose book level was below that indicated by their 'ability'. Such children, and others, sometimes took their books home for their parents to hear them read. Children who asked to do so were allowed so that they could more quickly reach the 'target' set for them by their teacher. This individual differentiation of 'progress' was allowed since, unlike mathematics, it did not need to be managed to keep stable groups. Children also read teacher-selected or approved books from the class collection or library.

The teachers of St. George's used a variety of reading materials including the Griffin and Dragon Pirate Stories, Wide Range Readers and Science Research Associates ('SRA'). Mr Gordon gave every child the Holborn reading test each year. Each child's record sheet, which he kept, was a graph of Reading Age against Chronological Age, with a straight line drawn through equal age values, that is, the defined mean values for the child population. He expected, and usually found, scores to run parallel with the line; for their reading 'development' to be at a constant rate. If the line of the graph went down 'the bells start ringing', and the teacher was alerted to try to 'push them on a bit'.

Children could be reading at any time of the day, on arrival, 'Get your books out for a bit of quiet reading', or having finished other work, particularly mathematics. A more specific reading time had been called 'quiet time' at Greenleigh; the first quarter of an hour of each afternoon. All classes in the doorless classrooms read quietly, for 'a nice calm start to the afternoon', after the dinner–hour excitement. Some teachers called this time 'USSR', as did some children. None of the latter I asked could decode it, and some of the former stumbled to produce Uninterrupted Sustained Silent Reading. They were uncertain of the origin of what one called, 'Some "new" educationalist's idea, from a Conference somewhere'.

At St. George's I found another version of USSR, introduced with the headteacher's sanction, at the suggestion of a teacher following an in-service course on reading run by a local authority advisor. Four times a week for twenty minutes, the children of the first and second years, and separately those of the third and fourth, read their books in the hall supervised by one teacher, whilst small numbers of children were heard reading by the other teachers in their classrooms. Those in the hall were 'independent readers'; those in the classrooms 'needed special help'. Most teachers thought it worthwhile for the latter but had doubts about the former. 'A bit of a farce'. The teacher in the hall was supposed to be reading too, 'it sets an example', but spent most of their time 'looking out for mischief'. Mr Gordon, the headteacher, whose first reaction to 'USSR' was to laugh, supervised in the hall initially, but felt the 'novelty value had worn off a bit since then'. In the hall, the children sat on the floor. or the stage. As I observed them, some were reading, others quietly talking or playing. As Mr Gordon put it 'when you actually saw what the children were doing under the tables (used for dinner time), it wasn't so good'. Even when reading in class, 'You've always got children who look out the window anyway and will pretend to be reading and aren't'. The effectiveness of USSR may have been doubted, but it was an expression of the importance of reading.

Much of what the children read were stories, some of which corresponded to the multiple realities of the story worlds of infants' reading (King, 1978). Many were of a *'real' world of human beings,* often about children, as in the Teasing of Mike in *Freckles* (Ginn, Level 6 Book 1, 1978). The *animal-humanoid world* was rarer than in infants' reading. Most animals were presented in only a slightly anthromorphic way. Their thoughts were sometimes reported, but they seldom spoke. The *traditional story-world* was not common, and represented by versions of folk tales, such as *The Boy Who Went to the North Wind,* where the wind talks. The teachers in Barker Lunn's (1984) national survey reported children to be reading silently to themselves as an activity only less frequently followed than mathematics computations. Whilst reading, children had access to a wide range of story worlds, poems as well as factual material, some of which they could reproduce in their own writing.

Writing as distinct from handwriting, was done in most lessons. 'Writing' in English took different forms. Children's understanding of their reading was assessed by their oral and written expression, by the completion of comprehension exercises associated with the different reading schemes. Their writing resources were in their reading books, but other writing required their being able to spell words. All the children at Greenleigh had dictionaries; small numbers (sometimes only one) were kept in each class at St. George's. Children, doubtful of spelling, might consult the dictionary or their teacher, who sometimes required them 'to give it a try' on a piece of paper before telling them, for writing in their 'word books'. Each class at St. George's was a set spelling test each week, and one English homework was to prepare for it, a list of words having been copied down in advance. Mistakes in a test or writing, in both schools, meant the children having to write corrections.

Comprehension and the skills of writing reproduction were an important part of English 'exercises' used extensively at St. George's, often based upon the Haydon Richards Junior English Series (1965). What counts as 'English' is as variable in secondary schools as it is in juniors. Wilkinson (1966) suggested a typology of Secondary English Teachers, one of which was teacher as proof reader. Teachers proof read children exercise scripts, often correcting in red. There was only one 'correct' answer to an exercise such as

Arrange the words in each sentence in the right order.
1. Trees oak on grow Acorns. (Haydon Richards Junior English Book Two).

In *creative writing*, children had scope to write acceptably different things. In teaching reading and handwriting, teachers demonstrated their own competence in these skills and were models for the children. They also read stories and poems to the children as a 'treat' at the end of the day or the week, sometimes as a serial. However, although children wrote poems and stories in their creative writing sessions, teachers did not demonstrate their competence to do so or provide models to follow. They provided the initial idea and structured its development by the children.

> *T:* This is going to be the most exciting story you've ever written. You're going to a palace. Perhaps Buckingham Palace. Or maybe 10 Downing Street. Who lives there?
> *Child:* The Prime Minister.
> *T:* Yes. Perhaps the White House. Where is that?
> *Child:* America.
> *T:* And who lives there?
> *Child:* The Prime Minister (others laugh).
> *T:* Well, not their prime minister, what's he called?
> *Child:* The President.
> *T:* You're going there for all sorts of things maybe to go to a party or even just as the dustman. Remember it's your own story so I want no talking while you do it.

When handwriting or writing for English exercises, presentation and spelling were important, but these were less important with creative writing.

> Don't worry about spelling and things just now. I'm not worried about the writing. Just the ideas.

An initial draft would be done in a jotter and a corrected version, in 'your best handwriting' and right spellings made later.

Discussions with the children often preceeded creative writing, and sometimes were activities in themselves, starting with an infants'-style Newstime ('did anyone do anything interesting over the weekend?'), or an item of national or local news, sometimes taken from a broadcast or recorded children's radio or television programme. 'Anyone know what happened in Yugoslavia yesterday?'.

All that the children read or heard had a cultural content, and they may have learnt and shared it in the process of learning to read, write, spell or punctuate. This incidental culture transmission was of general knowledge and sayings.

> The answers to the questions in this exercise may be found in your dictionary from words that begin with e, f, g, h, i, j, k or l.

> A haddock lives in the . . . . . and looks rather like a . . . . . .

> (Exercises from an Easy Dictionary)
> Right, first word (of the spelling test). 'Stitch'. A stitch in time saves nine.

Drama was the most infrequent of activities under the heading of English, some classes doing none. It had been timetabled as a separate activity for the fourth year at St. George's, but then abandoned. When it happened, drama usually took place in the hall often using recordings of schools' radio broadcasts, music and activity instructions, edited and complemented by the teacher.

4 School Work: Other Subjects

The 'basics', mathematics and English, were the most important work for both children and teachers. The other subjects of the curriculum, more often for the afternoons than the mornings, were more varied within and between the two case-study schools, an index of their relative importance.

Geography and History

At 'traditional' St. George's, geography and history were clearly defined. They were taught and learnt in all classes on the basis of whole class groups, that is, mixed ability groups, other than the third year streams. There was no concept of geography or history ability to form the basis of specialized groups, and the subjects were only timetabled if they were not taught by the class teacher, and so were sometimes followed irregularly and infrequently. It is not surprising that they were seldom given importance by the third year children, who also seldom named them as interesting.

The principal resources of most teachers were recently acquired texts of the Oxford New Geography and the Oxford Junior History, copies of which were available for the use of individual children, although not to keep as 'their own', as with their mathematics and English texts. These were often supplemented by material, prepared by the teachers, such as work cards. The skills of listening, reading and writing were important for the children's tasks, although some teachers included practical activities such as measuring for map making and visits in the local area, as well as drama (the murder of Julias Caesar — not by Shakespeare) and craft work, in making model villages and coats of arms. As may be expected, the content of both subjects was conspicuously Anglo-centric. The children were learning to be British if not English, as indeed they were, there being only three children of ethnic minorities in the school. (They may have thought of themselves as British or English, but were not thought so by the ethnic majority children, some of whom, their teachers reported, used what may be considered to be racist names for them.)

There was a measure of child-centredness in the texts sometimes starting with material involving everyday life and child characters. So the Celts were learnt about through the account of the life of the boy Briacan, of whom the text asks questions and to which he answers. History presented a set of story worlds, necessarily distanced from everyday life, being of the past. Geography, of the present, could start in a version of the here and now, with the topography of the fictional Granby's house, and the cleaning of Murkyville.

Although geography was well-defined at Greenleigh, history was more elusive. Both had been taught in the junior school before re-organization and the move to the new open-plan building. Mr Kirby introduced what at one time was called social studies and later environmental studies (both terms still having currency) and which were intended to incorporate history and geography. Recently, he had introduced the texts of the Outset Geography series. I suggested that this had 'squeezed history out a little bit'. He agreed. 'Well, yes, I think you are right. I think actually that history is not just squeezed out. History is difficult to identify in the school'. Some teachers regretted the loss of history, one expressing her feelings with a nostalgic pat on a pile of unused books by A.J. Unstead. The children knew what history was and that they didn't do it, although some of the things they were taught and learnt could be described as history.

Topics and Projects

At Greenleigh children worked on 'topics'. These were not timetabled on a school basis, although the subjects were prescribed by the headteacher. (Experienced teachers recalled how a former colleague had been reproved for making her own choice.) The whole class followed the same topic, for example, water, over a period of up to a term. Their resources were books, schools' television, commercial and teacher produced material. The end products were individual illustrated and written folders and a class display. In orthodox terms, the topic could be treated as a combined exercise in geography, science, creative writing, and the illusive history. Thus for 'water', children drew maps of rivers, did experiments on flotation, poems on rain and accounts of the cholera epidemic in 1832.

Some teachers at St. George's used a similar method for what they called 'class projects'. Others allowed the children to follow what were called 'personal projects', where the children had a degree of choice from a number of teacher categories, for example, nature or sports. The children's main resources were books from the library, the class collection or their own. The teachers would only approve a project if a child could show that sufficient or suitable books were available. Thus a girl could not do 'cartoons' because although she had books (of her own) of cartoons, there were no books *about* cartoons. Sometimes there was competition among the children for scarce resources, like the only book on ice-skating.

Teachers were well aware that some children copied material straight from books. 'Don't copy great chunks out — write in your own words'. But admitted they had difficulty in detecting plagiarisms, but sometimes guessed so from the style and grammar. 'Who's this you or the book? Be honest Amanda'. Amanda smiled at her detection when asked to fetch the book. 'Read the book, and do your own writing'. Some children were practiced paraphrasers. Tracey had used *How Wild Flowers Live* as her source. The words she deleted in her copying are in brackets.

Inside (the stem of) the plant there are many tubes. The tubes carry water and food to all parts of the plant. Wood is (also) made of many (of these) tubes.

Teachers limited the illustrative material children used. 'Pictures are lovely, but you should have writing to go with them'.

Children did their projects in designated and 'spare' time, having finished another activity. Mr Gordon, the headteacher of St. George's, was concerned about the copying that went on, but topics were convenient for teachers who felt the children, particularly the less able, got satisfaction in producing 'something of their own', 'nicely produced, in their best handwriting'. The third year children often named topics as their favourite thing done at school. None thought them important. Their enjoyment, by their own accounts, was in doing something of their own (constrained) choosing. A consequence was that the topics followed were different for boys and girls. In Miss Hunt's second year class, the girls' topics were, four on flowers, living things, cats, dress, birds, horses, winter sports, Guernsey, wild birds and hibernation. The boys were, two on sports, two on computers, two on the army, cars, human body, castles, aeroplanes, winter, mountaineering, animals in winter, football, tanks, prehistoric monsters. Miss Hunt was aware of these differences, but saw them as a 'natural' consequence of children following their interests — the major justification of 'personal projects'. The children saw these as natural differences too.

> *Boy:* There's a project on army and navy, and things like that don't interest girls really.
>
> *Boy:* We've got a travel project and that's more interesting for boys than girls.
>
> *Girl:* In nature (projects) girls really take it in because we've got soft hearts about animals and that, if they get killed, but boys they just laugh, girls have soft hearts and take care of animals.

Practical Subjects

Children followed a range of activities which in secondary schools, but not the two study schools, are called 'practical subjects'; art, craft, cookery and sometimes in this category, music. Together with physical education games, they involved little or no reading or writing. At St. George's, third year children often named art and craft as the thing they enjoyed most at school, but gave it little importance, because, as one boy said, 'not many people get jobs as artists'.

The activities of *art and craft*, followed in the afternoons, included drawing, painting, printing and pottery. Like infants' teachers, those of the younger children interpreted their products as indices of their maturity. Some children at Greenleigh were thought to be particularly 'artistic'; a quality sometimes set against their modest general 'ability'.

Art and craft were only timetabled when not taken by the class teacher. At Greenleigh, some of the children's mothers, some qualified teachers, took small groups of children in the bays outside the doorless classrooms. Mr Kirby, the headteacher, described himself as 'an art and craft person', and although grateful and encouraging about the mothers' help, felt the quality of work could be better. A kiln had been cold and unused since a teacher enthusiast left.

The activities were timetabled for the third and fourth years at St. George's and taken by the teacher 'in-charge' of art and craft, in the 'art and craft area'. This was a classroom-sized glazed and heated space between two classrooms added to the original building and the hall. Fourth years were timetabled for an afternoon, fortnightly, in half-classes, boys and girls separately, because 'they are interested in different things'. When they did pottery figures (the kiln was used), the girls' were in balletic poses, the boys' of sportsmen. Mrs Clark, the teacher, felt that some children, more often girls, found the activities therapeutic if they had 'problems' at home, having observed some kneading clay contentedly.

Small groups of children, at Greenleigh, both boys and girls, did *cookery*, in the bays supervised by mother-helpers. A similar arrangement had been tried at St. George's, but had stopped due to lack of space and hints of the mothers' problems of controlling the children in an area remote from the teacher. The cookers were disconnected and put under the platform in the hall.

Teachers took their own classes for *music* at Greenleigh, five of the eight being pianists, (a scarce skill at St. George's, of only two of the twelve). Schools' television and radio broadcasts were used, and by the third year, all children played recorders. Other instruments were learnt by some children, taught by peripatetic teachers. They found the children to be often from 'musical homes', with parents who played the piano and bought the children's instruments. No one thought the children's 'work' suffered when they missed mathematics or English lessons, for a violin or flute lesson. Most instrumentalists were in the top set for mathematics. A peripatetic teacher remarked on the preponderance of girls learning violin and woodwind, with only boys on brass. The former had become 'an effeminate thing'. 'Not a word they'd use'. The girl instrumentalists noted the absence of boys, and explained that, 'boys like doing what other boys do'.

Only first year teachers took their own classes for music at St. George's, which was timetabled for others with the 'music specialist' and the other pianist-teacher. Some children were taught instruments by peripatetic teachers using school-owned instruments. Children often gave up, they lacked 'stickability'. Girls 'stuck it' more often than boys, who would 'sooner be playing football'.

Science

All teachers taught science to class groups, but few were confident in doing so, often saying 'I'm not a scientist'. Although they taught the subjects, they never referred to themselves as mathematicians or geographers. Older teachers fondly recalled the nature study that preceded 'Science', and which found a small place in the new study and in projects. Mr Gordon at St. George's thought the children were being given 'a taste of science'. Mr Kirby at Greenleigh, whilst admitting he was not a 'specialist', was more ambitious, and wanted science to be given equal importance to mathematics and language work, a policy that the teachers reported with amused resignation. (Nationally, Barker Lunn (1984), found junior school teachers reporting science to be the eleventh most frequent activity of twenty-one investigated.) To this end he cannabalized copies of *Science from the Beginning* (Hampson and Evans, 1977) into work cards. Although sometimes a teacher would make them the basis of a lesson, children worked at them individually. The card was read, the pictures, text and questions copied, and the answers filled in

Put one word in each space.
1. Salt is . . . . . with rocks and soil.
2. Salt . . . . . in water. Rivers . . . . . . it

The teachers thought these were basically comprehension exercises, rather like those in English, and Mr Kirby had doubts about how much science the children learnt. The teachers felt that some had difficulty in doing the exercises. Those children who thought they found no difficulties, described them as 'just copying'.

Mr Kirby wanted children to 'find out about science for themselves', through the cards and practical work. His predecessor, with the help of advisors, had acquired 'piles' of science apparatus and materials to equip the new school, but this had been little used. Mr Kirby, with the help of a former member of staff, wrote work cards of experiments to be carried out by third and fourth year children, working in small groups with trays of apparatus and materials. Children's access to these exercises was governed by where they were in their Fletcher mathematics; the further they were on, the quicker and more often they did experiments. Science lessons were ability differentiated by mathematical ability.

Teachers at both schools were eclectic in their resources for science, using texts, television and their own work cards. Some used published material to the extent of reproducing whole unparaphrased sections in their notes for children. This material was child-centred to the extent of using some of the elements of story-worlds. In *Science Workshop* by Irene Finch, an anthropomorphized Tommy Tomato explains how a 'botanist' defines a fruit, differently to a cook. A child-centred anthropomorphism may have been involved in the material prepared by teachers.

Friction pushes (*sic*) against anything which is moving and tries (*sic*) to make it stop.
Compressed air likes (*sic*) to expand.

Science as the special province of scientists was stressed in published material and by teachers, who sometimes attributed remarkable importance to them.

Scientists must have done lots of experiments before they found out about how things float, because we've had boats for a very long time.

When some teachers departed from the details of published material, their modest descriptions of themselves as not being 'a scientist' were confirmed.

> Mrs Rose introduces the topic of blood by telling the puzzled children it is 'straw coloured'. The children are to write about blood using books from the library. A girl found one describing blood as red. 'That's only when it's exposed to the air', explains Mrs Rose.

During the course of the lesson the children consulted her about things they were reading, in which she said that the rh factor gave rise to 'blue babies', that veins are blue on the outside (the blood inside being straw coloured), and that most of Queen Victoria's sons died of haemophilia.

> Mr Richards had done science 'up to O-level'. He had prepared cards for the children's work. 'This week we are going to look at what the eye sees' He explains, 'the brain is like a large computer'. 'There isn't a wire connection, but? (Girl) 'Nerves'. 'Yes'.

He went on to talk about optical illusions, but not to explain them. Children did experiments following the instructions of his cards. No child I asked could explain 'optical illusion'. One boy with the card on the blind spot, thought it was an optical illusion. A girl could not understand the word 'kinematic' on her card. She couldn't find it in her dictionary, nor in the 'big one' she fetched from the staff room. Mr Richards found it and paraphrased. 'Things that seem to move, but not really'. (*Oxford Illustrated Dictionary*, 'Kinematic adj. Of motion considered abstractly without reference to force or mass'.) The girl wrote in her account, 'Kinematic means that things that appear to move but there not'. Later she said to her friend, 'This is the best science lesson we've ever had'. I reported this remark to Mr Richards, who agreed the children enjoyed doing the work, but, 'I don't know how much they get out of it'.

Not all lessons departed so much from orthodox science, but in no other subjects were the equivalent unorthodoxics and obscurities taught. No child was taught that nine nines are seventy-two or that Wolverhampton is the capital of England.

Religious Education

Religious education is the only subject (currently) required to be taught in maintained schools by law. In form and method the lessons at

Greenleigh were similar to those for geography, topics or some kind of English, following formally, the syllabus agreed by the Nossex local authority. The children read and were read to, wrote and illustrated, and acted *about* Christianity and the bible, in the way they did about the weather or flotation. The Christian festivals of Easter and Christmas were marked, with decorated classrooms for the latter, although not as splendid as in infants' schools. ('Musn't be too like the first school', was a teacher's response to my comment on her class's efforts.) Only occasionally was the Christian content extended.

> T: Right I put a little notice on the board (It says, 'Christmas is coming'.) Has Britain always been a Christian country?
> Girl: No.
> T: What was it before?
> Children: Jewish. Protestant. Roman Catholic.
> T: Begins with a p.
> Boy: Palestine.
> T: Pagan.
> Boy: Never heard of it.

The teachers of St. George's did not take religious education lessons; what they called 'the Vicars' did instead. St. George's was a large parish. The vicar, two curates and a retired clergyman took all the religious education at what was once the Church of England parish elementary school, and which now had assisted status. The teachers had mixed feelings about the arrangement. They were grateful to have a 'free' period, but concerned about the lessons they were not taking. The content had been 'very churchy', with the children reporting that they had been questioned about their having been christened and their attendance at church and Sunday school. Some of the teachers had drawn up a syllabus more acceptable to them, which the headteacher had negotiated with the clergy to accept in modified form.

The teaching methods of 'the vicars' was also of some concern. One was a trained teacher, but the others were 'learners'. No teacher observed a religious education lesson, but afterwards they could see the quality of the handwriting on the board, ('he needs to come to my handwriting lessons'), and note that the children's writing in their religious education books was never marked, and so (they thought) the writing and spelling were below their usual standard. The children confirmed that they could not read the writing on the board, and that it didn't matter if they did any 'work' because it was never marked. I was able to observe one lesson. The children's behaviour was more like that of playtime than in lessons with their own teacher, with more movement around the classroom, shouting out answers to questions and personal conversations. As after other religious education lessons, their teacher found them to have 'got a bit excited' and had to calm them down. One teacher who thought the lessons a waste of time, arranged to withdraw 'poor' readers for extra help with her.

The law also required a corporate act of worship each day in a school. At St. George's, the vicars took *school assembly* four days of the week, the headteacher the fifth. The teachers attended but were grateful not to be more active participants, except for the two pianists. They knew that in other schools it was common for teachers to conduct assemblies, as at Greenleigh. There, some were like infants' teachers (King, 1978) apprehensive about so public a performance. 'Alright if it's only the children there, but not in front of all the staff'. The teacher and her class prepared for their performance over a period of weeks, with activities similar to those of project work and English. Material was collected and created around a theme, secular rather than sacred, such as 'space' or 'food'. In addition to a hymn, the children gave instrumental performances, read their own work and others, and acted playlets of their own composition.

> Mrs Dandridge's assembly is on the theme of 'communications'. She looks concerned as she makes an aside to me, 'Panic stations'. The religious content is slight. After the readings, musical performances and playlet, the concluding prayer is 'Thank you God for communications'. On the way out of the hall, she smiles at me and wipes her brow, with the back of her hand, 'Phew!'.

Physical Education and Games

Physical education and games were, together with art and craft, commonly named as the things they enjoyed most in school by the third years of St. George's. In both schools, these activities were given little importance, even by those boys with ambitions to be professional footballers. Their status as school work was equivocal, physical education only 'a sort of work', and 'games' were also a playtime activity.

At Greenleigh physical education was taken in the hall. The children changed in the cloakrooms, separate for boys and girls, the former into white shorts the latter into black leotards, bare footed. At St. George's they changed together in the classroom into a variety of shorts, shirts and leotards, and plimsolls. The floors of the corridors and of the hall where they did physical education, were 'too dirty for bare feet'. Teachers did not do physical education, acting as models as they did for some other activities. They took their coats and cardigans off, and put on trainers or ballet slippers. They designated particular children to 'give a lead' in demonstrating an exercise or using the apparatus. These models were often members of the gymnastics clubs that met after school or dinner time, run by teachers, with some parents. These clubs also met for the same team sports that constituted 'games', on one afternoon a week, weather permitting. These were sex-differentiated with football and cricket for boys and netball and rounders for girls. (Some girls complained to me about not being able to play football.) School teams were entered in the Newbridge Middle School competitions. Boys and girls were taken to the swimming baths together, and at Greenleigh played mixed sex shinty.

French

When teachers talked of 'language work', it was synonymous with 'English', it did not include French. French had been taught to children from the age of eight in the junior schools of Newbridge, but in the middle schools only the fourth year learnt it. Nationally and locally, the experience of primary French had lead to its being less valued, there being no evidence that the extent of it influenced performance in secondary school (Burstall *et al*, 1974).

The fourth year followed, by local agreement, a 'Longman's-type' scheme. Even some of those teachers who, having attended special courses, taught the subject, doubted its worth, particularly for the 'less able', who have enough trouble with their own language'. Mr Gordon hoped the children of St. George's could go to their comprehensives and say "I like French". Mr Kirby thought that French, was or should be part of 'good primary school practice', and against local and national trend would have liked it taught throughout the school, indeed from the age of five.

Teachers at St. George's had only a vague concept of children having a special capacity to do French. It was thought to be related to their ability to do English, and to vary between individuals but to be fairly stable. Children were initially allocated to one of three sets on the basis of their last year's performance in English, their reading ages and verbal reasoning quotient. Some changes were made after a few weeks, 'when they'd settled down' and 'showed what they could do'. Not surprisingly, 73 per cent of children had the same set status for English and French, no child being in a set one and a set three.

Subjects of the Curriculum

The sum of the subjects did not define the curriculum. The subjects were defined by the time-table, text and exercise book, but teaching and learning happened without these. The parents at both schools were told that the children would receive sex-education, to allow them to withdraw the children. The children were not told they were receiving sex-education when it occurred. No text or exercise book was so labelled. The children of Greenleigh received what their headteacher called personal, social and moral education, but no child knew so. 'What was that?' I asked a boy after a class discussion of 'my fears'. 'Sometimes we just have a chat'.

5   Classroom Control

The social structure of a classroom consists of the repeated patterns of behaviour of the teacher and children. Social structures have a dual quality. The *social order* of repeated behaviours is the outcome of the exercise of *social control*. Teachers are the main agents of social control, through the exercise of *power*. To paraphrase Weber's (1964) definition to fit the classroom situation, 'Power is the chance of a teacher realizing her own will against the resistance of the children'. The will of most teachers was realized, in that there was usually classroom order to their general satisfaction.

The teachers had two purposes in the exercise of social control to produce classroom social order; as an end in itself or as a means to an end. Orderliness and the required behaviour of the children could be valued for its own sake. This is an aspect of what Durkheim (1961) called *moral education*.

> Discipline '. . . is not a simple device for solving superficial peace in the classroom − a device for allowing work to roll on tranquilly. It is the morality of the classroom'.

But for the teachers of Greenleigh and St. George's, order and control were more important as means to an end, getting the work done. This was consonant with their professional ideology of the primacy of work.

The methods used by teachers to control children's behaviour were in accord with another element of their ideology; the end of innocence. Children were defined as being responsible for their own behaviour and knew when they were 'not behaving themselves'. These methods varied according to the nature of the work being done, and the material conditions in which it was being carried out. Although children spent most of their time working in classrooms, being at school also meant activities outside, in corridors and playground. The nature of the social order of these places was different to that of classrooms, but was also the outcome of social control.

Methods of Classroom Control

When teachers controlled children's behaviour to accord with conventional politeness, such behaviour was being intrinsically valued — the 'morality of the classroom' (Durkheim, 1961).

> If you can't say something nice, don't say it. Philip, don't talk while I'm talking please, it's very rude.

However, 'good behaviour' was given a greater extrinsic value in allowing 'work to roll on tranquilly' (Durkheim, 1961).

> Some of you are being very rude again when I'm hearing someone read.

> You should finish your work if you don't chat and do silly things.

Infants' teachers typically control their younger children using *oblique* methods (King, 1978). 'Someone's being silly'. Children defined as being innocent in the intention of their (teacher) unacceptable behaviour were not directly rebuked. The teacher of juniors did not attribute such innocence to older children, whose control was more *direct*.

> Right, that's enough of this noise. Books out ready to start.

Whereas infants' teachers typically praised 'good' behaviour and seldom directly blamed 'bad', juniors' teachers' balance of *praise and blame* shifted to the latter. Children were defined as being responsible for their own behaviour.

> Carl, stop it. You are being deliberately naughty.

For mildly unacceptable behaviour *semi-oblique* control could be used.

> There's always someone who keeps the table waiting, Simon.

As with infants' teachers, this could take the form of a *no need to answer question*.

> Louise, why are you talking? (Not Louise, stop talking). You've got lots to correct. Do you know why? Because you chatter.

Request — orders, were also semi-oblique.

Right Janie, would you like to put the books on my table.

Humour could be used in semi-oblique ways in correcting work.

I think you got slightly confused. I think you started to get tired.

Jokes were more direct.

He'd forget his head if it wasn't screwed on. Wake up Joseph, it's not bed-time yet.

Teachers referred to their own *emotional state* in expressing disapproval.

I'm sorry, but that will not do. You know I don't like noise. Look, I'm fed up with you Robin Hill. Go and sit over there.

More direct was the teachers' *threatening their own crossness.*

There are some people who will make me really cross in a minute. I think I will lose my temper soon.

With *reference control,* children were reminded of significant relationships, including those of authority, as in *headteacher reference control.*

Danny, do you want to be working outside Mr Gordon's room?

Parent reference control was used less often than in the infants'.

What would your mum say about being untidy? I saw her the other day.

Age reference control was quite common.

Please don't be a baby. Do grow up. You are ten years old, and you should be able to look after your own ruler.

Sex reference control was rare.

Right boys, mothers' meeting's over (Man teacher). Ann, what is this a mothers' meeting? (Woman teacher)

Although the different sets and streams had different *ability — status* this was never used for control purposes, as in secondary schools ('I don't expect 3A to behave like this').

As in infants' classrooms, teachers used both *private and public voices,* with the latter predominating. Private voice was addressed to one or a small group of children, and could be heard only by them. Public could be used with larger groups or the whole class, but even so when addressed to one or a few, all could hear, so allowing what Kounin (1970) calls 'ripple effects'.

Somebody's talking, Craig. (They all go quiet).

The children learnt to interpret the various *teacher voices*. Five were common, each with distinctive tone, delivery, accompanying facial expression, and meanings above those of the actual phrases spoken. Three were similar to those used by infants' teachers (King, 1978).

'I'm being very patient with you' voice; 'Listen to me, I'm saying something important', voice 'Sorrowful, you're not pleasing me', voice.

Two were more direct.

'Do as I say, no nonsense' voice; 'I know what you're up to, you're not fooling me' voice.

Infants' teachers used pairs of words in a dichotomized way, signalling approval or disapproval (King, 1968). Junior teachers occasionally used silly/sensible and quiet/noisy, but the primacy of work showed in their use of quick/slow and careful/careless.

You'll have to be quicker than this Adrian, you're too slow to catch a cold. Too many careless mistakes. Be more careful.

For some children, there was a problem in being quick enough without being careless.

I could get it right, if I didn't have to rush so much.

The language of social control was often strongly dependent upon the context for understanding. This was so in the use of *naming*. 'Joanne' could mean, stop talking, bring your book to me or many other things. The uses of first and surname, 'Joanne Sedley', signalled strong disapproval, whilst adult titles, 'Come along Miss Sedley', signalled mild but amused disapproval, evoking embarrassed smiles from the children.

The language of control could be condensed to a single word or sound. In the right context, with the appropriate facial and vocal expression, and body attitude, 'Now' or 'Eh' could produce silence. Even the teacher stopping talking and staring hard at an offender, could produce the desired effect. *Eye-Scanning and contact*, 'Keeping an eye on them', was used but less often than with infants' teachers, who with typical obliqueness, more often controlled with a wordless look (King, 1978). Teachers would look if a word or movement caught their attention, and children would reciprocate her gaze, not with the guilty give-away look typical of infants, but often with a wry or embarrassed smile of acknowledgement of being caught.

In his theory of codes, Bernstein (1975) hypothesized that an elaborated code forms the basis of the language of learning. However, the language of classroom control comes closer to his hypothesized restricted code: lexically and syntactically simple, its meaning often implicit and dependent on extra-verbal signals, context bound and expressing the positional authority of the teacher. This language was used almost exclusively by teachers. Children did not have to learn to encode it, but only to decode it. Given that order and teacher's will generally prevailed, they must have decoded successsfully.

Control and Assessment of Behaviour

The teacher's exercise of control was also an assessment of children's behaviour. Every comment defined whether the behaviour was acceptable, good or bad, and often whose behaviour it was. The control would not have been effective if the children could not similarly define behaviour acceptable to their teacher, and learn which children met her expectations. In their terms, unacceptable behaviour was, 'mucking about', 'showing off'.

Third years were presented with a list of the names of the children in their class, and asked to tick those 'who sometimes don't behave themselves', with the reminder 'Tick yourself if you think you ought to'. About half the children in each class reported they sometimes misbehaved, and with the exception of the bottom stream of St. George's, boys did so more often than girls. The same pattern was found to their opinions of other children's behaviour. Because of the small numbers involved, it is not possible to assign statistical significance to these differences, but they may be said to have social significance, in that some girls expressed the view (in interviews) that boys were less well behaved.

Correlations between the boys' and girls' assessments were statistically significant, showing them to be in good agreement on what was good and bad behaviour, and who was well or badly behaved (table 1).

Table 1: Product-moment correlations, boys' and girls' assessments of others who 'Sometimes don't behave themselves'

	Greenleigh			St. George's	
	r	(n)		r	(n)
Mixed-ability group I	0.86	(27)	Top Stream	0.87	(35)
Mixed-ability group II	0.88	(27)	Middle Stream	0.79	(24)
			Bottom Stream	0.64	(14)

(All correlations statistically significant at the 5 per cent level or higher by t test)

A number of studies (Douglas, 1964; Kelmer-Pringle, 1966) have shown teachers to assess boys' behaviour less favourably than girls'. With the exception of one teacher (concerned at the prospect of teaching an older class for the first time), none at Greenleigh expressed the view that boys' behaviour was poorer. Indeed, some teachers thought some boys a little 'soft'. (This was similar to the situation in the middle class infants' school I studied.) At St. George's, several teachers expressed the view that boys were 'more trouble' than girls. I saw an opportunity to quantify this from the end of year reports, which included the teacher's comment on 'general behaviour'. (It is significant that no such comment was codified on the Greenleigh report — a point I will return to in chapter 6.) However, because of teachers' industrial action, they decided (on Union advice) not to complete reports. Fortunately, the three third year teachers generously agreed to complete a version for me. Methodologically, this was an improvement on the 'real thing', in that they made their assessments without taking into account any anticipated reception of parents and children.

I classified their comments into positive ('good throughout the year'), mixed or neutral ('fairly good can be easily distracted'), or negative ('Taken a time to settle in. "Shows off"'). As with the children, their teachers gave more favourable assessments to girls, although the small numbers involved do not allow statistical significance to be assigned. However, the repeated pattern of results, and the consciousness of these sex-differences by teachers and children, suggest they are socially significant.

Furthermore, there was very good agreement, in general terms, between the children and their teachers' assessments. Each child was given a score of the number of other children in the class who thought he or she 'sometimes did not behave themselves' — their behaviour status. The teachers' assessments were given an arbitrary score; positive 3, mixed or neutral 2, negative 1. The correlations between the children's and their teacher's assessments were statistically significant (table 2).

The social significance is that these classes were, in Durkheim's (1961) terms, morally consensual. Teachers and children agreed on what was good or bad behaviour, and who was well or badly behaved. In Weber's

Table 2: Product-moment correlations between children's assessments of others 'Sometimes don't behave themselves' and teachers' assessments of 'general conduct' (St. George's)

Stream	Top	Middle	Bottom
r (n)	− 0.88 (35)	− 0.55 (24)	− 0.67 (14)

(All correlations statistically significant at the 5 per cent level or higher by t test. For interpretation purposes the sign of correlation should be reversed.)

(1947) terms, the children legitimized the teacher's power in controlling them, so conferring authority. The nature of their legitimation was largely traditional — children do as teachers tell them. A boy complained to me, 'You got to do what teacher tells you'. A girl rejoined, 'Oh, why'd you come to school'.

Curriculum, Pedagogy and Control

The American psychologist Phillip Jackson was an exponent of the use of interaction analysis in classroom research, in which a trained observer completes a pre-coded schedule of observations of specific elements of behaviour of a small number of children for short periods of time, (as little as 10 second intervals for 10 minutes). When Jackson (1968) laid aside his schedule to make unstructured observations, he saw that children had to learn more than the subjects taught to succeed. For example, the 'correct' answer had to be given in the 'correct' way. This element he called *'the hidden curriculum'* a dramatic but nonsensical term, since no teacher hides it and it is not hidden from the children.

The forms of classroom control described so far constitute a 'hidden curriculum'.

I heard what you said, but put your hand up when you want to answer a question.

However, the teaching and learning of the manifest curriculum of chapters 3 and 4 were forms of social control, the core of the social order of the classroom — work. The different kinds of work involved different relationships between teacher and taught. The subjects of the curriculum not only constitute discrete provinces of meaning, but different social structures, whose orders may be maintained by different forms of control. Differences in teaching method, pedagogy, of the same subject also create different structures with different social controls.

Mathematics at St. George's was based on whole class teaching with each child given the same task. Teachers varied in how much talk between the children was legitimate. Silence was rare, and some allowed talk as a part of 'helping' stopping short of telling the answers, 'cheating'.

The Fletcher scheme at Greenleigh involved more talking. Teachers 'discussed' the next section of work with a group, whilst another group discussed their task or performed a practical exercise. The teacher could not hear all the talk and classified some as not being legitimate on the basis of other clues. Although mathematics was the activity the children most enjoyed, any talk accompanied by laughter was suspect, and the children laughing would look to see if the teacher had heard. Talk between children was important in maintaining the group defined as of similar mathematical ability, particularly if a member had to 'catch up', sometimes after an absence. The opportunity for 'helping' to become 'copying' or cheating, was taken by some children. One girl told me she had fed the wrong answers to another who had 'pestered' her.

The many kinds of 'English' were controlled in different ways. As with mathematics at 'traditional' St. George's, class teaching with individual tasks did not require talk between children.

> Now you're each writing your own story, so there's no need for any talking.

At Greenleigh, 'discussions' were often a part of English than at St. George's. When a group talked among themselves, the teacher, as in Fletcher mathematics, had to judge if the talk was legitimate (no laughing), assessing the later report made by the group or a delegate ('spokesperson').

Drama provided scope for 'silly' behaviour. The first year secondary school boys in Beynon's study (1985) took the opportunity to 'express' themselves in ways unacceptable to their drama teacher. Drama was rare at St. George's. It had been timetabled for third and fourth year's, but the teacher had abandoned it because of the behaviour, particularly of the boys, who she said turned everything said into a 'double entendre'.

Music gave the opportunity for some (more often boys) to make non-musical sounds for their amusement, opportunities rarely taken at Greenleigh. The materials of art and craft, especially paint and water, could be put to 'mucking about' purposes. At St. George's, the fourth year half-classes were separate for boys and girls, not only because 'they are interested in different things' (chapter 4), but also because of the boys' behaviour. Girls confirmed their teacher's view saying that boys used to make fun of the girls' work. Not all the activities in physical education were part of the lesson, with mock boxing and pretend kicking by some boys (especially at St. George's), and ballet poses, by some girls. In the excitement of the game, the children were allowed to come closer to shouting than in any indoor activity.

Physical Arrangements, Material Conditions and Control

All human interaction takes place in material spaces which constrain actions. Human beings are themselves material objects and can't ordinarily walk through walls. The material conditions of school and classsroom, and the distribution of teachers and children in the spaces available, contribute to the relationships they make, and the forms of control used to maintain these social structures.

The physical arrangements for the class teaching commonly used in 'traditional' St. George's, was for the children to sit at desks or tables in parallel rows, facing the teacher and blackboard; what critics of the style call 'serried ranks'. This was to direct the children's attention to the teacher.

Right. Look at me. I want to see thirty pairs of eyes.

In class teaching, the children followed the same tasks individually, and although sometimes allowed to 'help' one another, were otherwise not supposed to talk. However, they did so, often undetected by not looking at one another, or when reading, cupping their faces in their hands. Working groups, common at Greenleigh for mathematics and other subjects, involved the children sitting around an arrangement of tables, to allow them to talk. Teachers had to judge the talk's legitimacy; no laughing or giggling. Control by eye-scanning and contact was used less often, since the children faced different directions.

In both schools, teachers managed the relationships between children by controlling seating.

Sean, you're not good for David. Bring your work here by me.

Moving children (more often boys) defined as naughty, closer to the teacher's table had two consequences. The intention was to 'keep an eye' on their behaviour, which if naughty was easily observed, so confirming the definition of the child's naughtiness. Similar behaviour in other parts of the room was not noticed or commented on. An unintended consequence was that the repositioned child could talk to the children waiting in a queue by the teacher's table, again, confirming the definition of their being naughty.

Teachers had autonomy in the arrangement of furniture and the disposition of children within a classroom, but were constrained in which classroom they taught. At Greenleigh, with the exception of mathematics most subjects were taught by the same class teacher in the same room. The more extensive use of setting at St. George's lead to children changing rooms during the day with greater movement around the corridors between lessons leading to jams in the narrower spaces. As I observed this, one teacher remarked, 'You take your life in your hands standing here.' On another occasion Mr Gordon, the headteacher, saw and greeted me with, 'Hullo, come to sample the chaos?' There were no explicit rules about moving from room to room, such as, keep to the left. The teachers were unsure who was responsible for the behaviour of the children, the teacher they were leaving or the one they were going to. Mr Gordon, acknowledged the problem and thought the 'geography' of the building was partly responsible, but also blamed the teachers.

> There are too many teachers, in spite of me saying otherwise, who don't really want to accept responsibility. I mean we (*sic*) said to them, 'Well, you should be standing in the door so you can see the length of the corridor'.

The teachers were usually busy accounting for the arrivals, 'Who's here? Who are we waiting for?' Some phased the departure of children to relieve the crush outside the door. 'Mrs Price's set, off you go. Girls first. Now boys'. Phased exits were also used in St. George's at break and dinner times, and at the end of the day.

> Right, let's see who wants to go home. Sit up straight. No talking. Alright, I don't mind, I'm in no hurry to go. O.K. now. Rachel's row.

These were good examples of what Waller (1932) called the *principle of least interest:* 'in cooperative activity, the person with less interest (the teacher in this case) controls it'.

Before they moved into the new building, the teachers at Greenleigh were apprehensive of teaching in an open plan school, and even after ten years some wished to 'have some doors put on'. The former Newbridge local education authority had built three open plan primary schools in the time before reorganization. Although the teachers were shown plans of the buildings and asked to comment, the decision on the design was not theirs. At the time of the 1972 survey, a new headteacher had just arrived at the old school. He left and was succeeded by Mr Kirby within a year, partly because of his not liking the open plan proposal, predicting, in the memory of one teacher, 'chaos'. Mr Kirby was enthusiastic and made the concept of 'openness' part of his educational thinking.

The material conditions of a school constrain actions, but do not determine them. In their study of open plan schools. Bennet, Andreae, Hegarty and Wade (1980) found that the same design of school could be organized in quite different ways. Greenleigh had been organized differently, with mixed age classes, until a recent fall in numbers. For the teachers, the meaning of being open plan was putting a premium on quiet working. This was generally fulfilled to the satisfaction of teachers and headteachers. The raised voice of a colleague in another class could sometimes be heard, and occasionally children working in the corridors would be reproved by another class's teacher. Some teachers arranged the furniture so that children would not be distracted by things going on outside the classroom.

Mr Kirby observed that when a teacher was heard shouting, 'everybody tends to huddle a little bit more over themselves, and actually are quiet too'; another ripple effect (Kounin, 1970). He recalled an incident that showed that the low sound insulation could lead to more quiet.

> On one occasion I found a boy doing something and gave him a wallop with my slipper at the top end of the school, and it echoed through the school, and it had a devastating effect, like a nuclear bomb exploding. And it had for a long time, I mean not just for a few moments, a long lasting effect. If I now went into school and was to raise my voice ... I would feel it would be heard.

One difference in teacher's classroom control between the two schools may have been related to different material conditions; children working outside the classroom. At St. George's individuals were sent out if they behaved badly. 'Right if you won't listen to what I say, you can take your work outside'. There, they were sometimes seen by the headteacher, and to maximize the possibility, sometimes sent to work outside his office door. At Greenleigh, individuals were sent, and sometimes asked to work outside, not because of their bad behaviour, but when the teacher trusted them to work adequately without her seeing and helping.

Control Outside the Classroom

Children were not only outside classrooms when moving between classes, but also at break and dinner times, before and after school, and were controlled by agents other than their class teachers, by other methods.

Teachers saw playtime as having a cathartic function, 'let off steam a bit', as do infants' teachers (King, 1978). It was defined as a time for behaviour not allowed in the classroom.

> We don't want any names called out here. Save it till playtime.
> Zena, fashion-talk at playtime please.

The playground was the place for French skipping, conkers and other games in season and vogue. Each day 'the duty teacher' was required (by the headteacher) to be in the playground before school started to blow a whistle to bring all the activity to halt, and supervise the children's lining up and entry into school, a process repeated at the morning and afternoon breaks, and dinner time. The duty teacher at Greenleigh could supervise the children's behaviour by standing on the path outside the school, which gave a view of the whole playground with only one small blind-spot. A whistle or call could quickly stop or correct misbehaviour. The play areas of St. George's were on two sides of the buildings, with many blind-spots from any angle. The whistle might have to be blown more than once to stop anything.

Prefects' duties included playground supervision. These were fourth year children, chosen by the headteacher and their teachers because they were, in the view of both choosers and chosen, 'sensible'. They also patrolled areas inside the school, including the toilets and cloakrooms. At Greenleigh, roughly equal numbers of boys and girls were prefects, but of the twenty five at St. George's, seventeen were girls. There had been an equal number of boys, but by the account of their teachers, many had 'dropped out', because being a prefect had little status and few privileges, they 'got fed up with bossing others about' and lost popularity with the other boys. I asked two girl-duty prefects where the third was — a boy. 'Playing football, I expect' was the contemptuous reply.

This sex-inbalance meant it was common to see a determined girl prefect lugging an equally large resisting boy into the school, where, if seen, he would be dealt with by the duty teacher, the head or the deputy headteacher. At the mid-day break, dinner ladies supervised the playground. Their relation to the prefects was unclear to both, but they could and did refer children to the headteacher.

Headteachers of maintained schools are legally responsible for discipline. They held the ultimate sanction in the cane (now illegal). No children had been caned at Greenleigh by Mr Kirby. Mr Gordon at St. George's had caned two boys in eight years, but 'slippered' more. Corporal punishment was the 'last resort'.

> The first time they see me I note the name of the child and date, and what's happened, what I've said, and what I've promised. If I've said I'll smack their bottom the next time, if there's a next time, I will, and that's recorded as well.

The children's response to punishment was:

> As long as you're fair and seen to be fair — the boys' attitude is that it's a fair cop.

The few boys who I spoke to who had the 'talking to', were amused at getting off so lightly. Mr Gordon knew this could happen.

> Some will get a good talking to and dissolve into tears. Others will be laughing their heads off once they get outside the door.

On the deterrent effect of caning, *pour encourager les autres,* Mr Gordon thought, 'your reputation lasts about four years'.

At Greenleigh, Mr Kirby conducted an assembly to all the children and staff each Friday afternoon, reviewing the week to 'clean the slate ready for Monday'. This included reports of bad behaviour made by prefects without naming culprits, because, 'they know who they are'. Children were urged to make other reports at the assembly or other times, 'tell the prefects, tell your teacher, tell me'. Mr Kirby agreed with my suggestion that this was an attempt to create a moral community, but did not think that their reporting others' bad behaviour was 'telling tales in that sort of way'. A consequence was that the child making the report was reproved for allowing the bad behaviour to happen. 'What did you do about it?' 'Nothing', was not an acceptable reply.

The exercise of social control usually has a tenuous quality, since power depends on the probability of compliance with rules to create order. Most teachers, most of the time, were confident that their will would prevail, and generally their expectations were fulfilled.

6   Typifications: 'Children in this School', Gender, Age and Ability

Junior teachers' professional ideology is based upon a definition of the nature of children of a particular age and of their learning, what in commentaries is often called 'the child'. This abstraction is a generalization about children; qualities shared by most of them, but not necessarily possessed by every individual. These subjective generalizations are ways of making sense of situations, a process Schutz (1932, 1972) called *typification*. For Weber (1968), the task of the sociologist was to delineate *social types*. 'Junior school children' constitute a social type. Like the typifications made in everyday life, social types are generalizations about the social actions of individuals in defined social conditions; in the example being followed here, children of a particular age attending school. The delineation of social types must be based upon the study of individuals' behaviour in certain situations, but the understanding and explanation of typical behaviour, should be informed by the typifications of the participants.

Explaining why teachers and children behave as they do, requires an understanding of their purposes in so behaving, what Weber called *Verstehen*. Thus the delineation of the social types of junior school teacher and junior school pupil, must take into account their relevant typifications. The account of classroom control (chapter 5) has already been presented through this process.

Like infants' teachers (King, 1978), those of juniors hold a set of typifications at different levels of generality. At the highest level they typify 'juniors', a definition consonant with their professional recipe ideology (chapter 2). Next, they typify 'children in this school' often effectively, 'the children I teach'. Children are typified as of a particular age, 'first years', 'second years' etc, and as 'boys' and 'girls'. They may also be typified as of a particular ability cohort, 'top set', 'remedial'. These are generalizations about groups of children that apply (in the teachers' view) to most but not necessarily to all. At the most specific level, each child was typified. These typifications were constructed by the teachers out of their everyday experience with the children concerned, representing what was 'real' for them.

'Children in this School' Greenleigh

Teachers at Greenleigh shared a definition of 'children in this school' which in orthodox terms was generally favourable. They were well-behaved and got on with their work, which was of a 'good standard'. The five who were interviewed in 1972 before re-organization felt that the children had not much changed since then. This was confirmed by the record of their views. Perhaps their long experience of the children lead them to define then as 'normal' in some general sense. Certainly, their new colleagues were more appreciative, making comparisons with other schools. Mrs Alison had taught in a country school of 'rather lumpy' children, 'but these are no trouble, a joy to work with'. She felt she could leave them to work alone in the classroom or corridor, knowing they would be just as quiet and industrious in her absence. Mrs Batholomew had been a supply teacher in several Newbridge schools and felt fortunate to be teaching at Greenleigh. She too found she could leave them, trusting them to behave. She allowed them to change for and shower after physical education, unsupervised. 'They're marvellous really. Not me' (placing an excluding hand on her chest).

This favourable definition was based on the teachers' day to day experience, confirmed by my observations. The children were generally quiet and conventionally polite towards adults and one another in school. They were tidy about the school, picking dropped things up without being told. I asked a girl if it were her job to tidy up, as she was doing. 'No, it's just something that should be done'. Mr Kirby the headteacher, pointed out that the school was in as good a decorative state as when it opened eight years before, 'no marks, no graffiti'. He attributed this to standards of behaviour that had been set for the children. The teachers explained the children's favourable characteristics in terms of the catchment area, the children's homes and families.

Although Mr Kirby thought 'we are very fortunate in our catchment area' teachers were more specific. Parents were 'concerned' and 'co-operative', they bought their children 'the right toys and the right books, to help them get on'. They were 'caring' parents providing a stable home background, 'materially and morally sound'. They talked to and encouraged their children, and controlled which programmes they watched on television.

How did the teachers come to define the children's homes and families in this way? Unlike those of infants, parents did not usually bring their children into the classroom in the morning or fetch them in the afternoon. They were seen and talked to at arranged meetings and, occasionally, more informally. The five long-serving teachers lived in the locality and had some parents as neighbours (even next door). In some cases they had even taught the parents at the former junior school. They had a store of local knowledge, sometimes shared in staffroom conversations. however, their pedagogy also made such knowledge available. 'News time' was not as common as in infants' schools, but 'who did something interesting over the weekend?' evoked accounts of country walks and visits to exhibitions and museums. The practice of children keeping a 'personally written diary' had only just been discontinued. In one teacher's recollection they provided insights into the home lives of the children that bordered on the indiscreet. 'We didn't want to know whose mother puts on more scent when the milkman comes'. Discussions relating topics to their own experiences lead to children reporting which parent was 'nagging' the other to give up smoking and whose father did all the weekend washing-up.

In the 1972 survey, teachers described the children's home backgrounds are 'mostly middle class', and they repeated the use of the class terminology when asked eleven years later. One of the more recent appointees said that in general the parents 'are your classic upper middle class types'. From information provided by the headteacher, 54 per cent of the children had fathers with non-manual occupations; a majority, but not overwhelmingly so, of middle class occupations. The longer experienced teachers knew that some fathers had manual jobs including baker's roundsman and lorry driver, but felt differences in background, on this account, made little difference to the children, except perhaps the incidence of local accents. They also knew which children lived in the diminishing number of council houses, and felt that like social class, housing class made little difference to the children's favourable presenting culture. This situation was very similar to that in one of the infants' schools of my earlier study (King, 1978). At Langley school, just over half of the fathers had non-manual occupations, but teachers defined 'children in this school' as being middle class. The headteacher actually said on my first visit, 'we have 75 per cent professional families'. In a study of Scottish junior schools, Nash (1973) found that teachers making favourable assessments of *individual* children, sometimes incorrectly defined them as having middle class parents. When teachers define the collectivity of 'children in this school' favourably, they tend to overestimate their middle classness.

The experienced teachers' view that the children and their background had changed little in a decade was confirmed by the 1971 and 1981 Census returns. The proportion of owner occupiers had increased a little from 81 to 85 per cent, and that of council house tenants fell from 11 to 7 per cent, due to privatization. The percentage of economically active males in each of the Registrar General's social class occupational categories remained virtually unchanged; professional 4, managerial 19, other non-manual 40, skilled manual 25, semi-skilled manual 9, unskilled manual 3. Unemployment had increased from 5 to 8 per cent; a national and local Newbridge trend. Teachers were aware of their being more children from 'broken homes'; the percentage of single parents of all parents with dependent children ('One parent families') had increased from 10 to 16 per cent; again a local and national trend. However, the teachers did not think the children concerned were necessarily disadvantaged by changes in family structure and composition. 'One boy seems very pleased to have two dads'.

'Children in this School' St. George's

The teachers at Greenleigh typified 'children in this school' consensually; they held a common definition and evaluation. Those at St. George's were less clear and more variable. With the exception of mathematics, when a teacher at Greenleigh taught a class she was dealing with a representative sample of the children in the school of a particular age, a group that she would teach most of the time. This was so for few teachers at St. George's. The use of setting and specialist teachers meant that a child could be taught by as many as four teachers in a day, and a teacher take four or more different groups of children, varying by age, sex and 'ability'. To the extent that there was a consensual view it was that they were 'ordinary children', 'a bit bouncy', 'all right once you get them settled down'. These reservations about their behaviour were acknowledged by Mr Gordon the headteacher. 'By and large the children's behaviour is regarded as being sort of acceptable'. In the *Information for Parents* brochure, a half-page section on 'Discipline and punishment' stated that 'Violent behaviour will not be tolerated', with details of the punishment given for 'persistent misconduct' and 'serious cases of indiscipline'. No such references were made in the information for parents at Greenleigh.

In the 1972 survey, the teachers of the 5–11 St. George's defined the children as being, 'pleasant and generally well-behaved'. Only one teacher remained from that time but two others were appointed soon after. The three agreed that the children had changed, that 'standards have gone down a bit'. They were unsure how to explain this, suggesting that children in general were changing, but no such observation was made at Greenleigh.

The staff of 1972 had described the children's parents as 'mainly middle class', and 'lower middle and upper working class'. Slightly less than half the fathers had non-manual occupations, 47 per cent, but in 1983 this had fallen to 35 per cent. Teachers continued to use class terminology in defining the children's home backgrounds. 'Very mixed really. Some middle class'. Because few teaching groups were representative of the children as a whole, teachers could define the children they taught most often, in different ways particularly in the streamed third year. It is well-established that middle class children tend to be statistically over-represented in top streams, a consequence of the relationship between the acquisition of measured intelligence and social class (Douglas, 1964; Jackson, 1964). The top stream class teacher described their parents as 'mainly middle class'; 63 per cent of the fathers had non-manual occupations. The middle stream teacher referred to 'mainly working class parents'; 27 per cent of fathers had non-manual jobs. More than half the children of the bottom stream were cared for by their mothers alone; all the known fathers' occupations were manual. Their teacher described these backgrounds as 'poor' and 'deprived'.

Mr Gordon knew the parents better than any teacher. Before reorganization, the school had a defined catchment area, and children generally went from the infants' to the junior department at seven-years-of-age. The new middle school had no associated first school and therefore no catchment area. Since the 1980 Education Act, no school has a legal catchment area, since parents have been allowed greater choice of their children's school. According to most headteachers of Newbridge schools, this lead to little change and some of them still talked (sometimes with a rather coy smile) of their catchment area. The 1980 Act meant that all parents of rising eight-year-olds could choose to send their children to St. George's, and Mr Gordon spent much of his time on their recruitment, spending at least half an hour with each interested parent, talking and touring the school.

He classified parents into two main groups: the terrace house people and the estate people. The former referred to the older owner-occupied houses around the school. Mr Gordon found, 'it's surprising how many parents and grand-parents went to this school. It seemed the natural thing to do and they've always stayed in the St. George's area'. These were 'hard times' for some of these geographically and socially immobile families, with more unemployment and more children claiming free meals. (Nineteen per cent of those staying for dinner: twice the proportion to that at Greenleigh.) In most school classes it was possible to see a few children poorly dressed. School uniform was compulsory (the parents having agreed on the policy) at Greenleigh, but optional at St. George's, and worn, with varying degrees of completeness, by the majority of children. Whereas no child wore trainers, non-flat heeled shoes or heavy boots at Greenleigh, these were common at St. George's, and girls' earrings as common as they were rare at Greenleigh. No Greenleigh child lacked the full physical education kit, but at St. George's teachers sometimes loaned lost property items to children without kit. Changing for physical education revealed the dirty feet of a few children at St. George's.

The 'estate' parents were from a modern development of mainly semi-detached houses. Mr Gordon contrasted them with those from the terraces, as being 'on the move', not just socially but geographically too, often changing house, sometimes as a consequence of 'unstable' family life (in contrast to the terrace families). Teachers at Greenleigh recognized some children had experienced the separation, divorce and re-marriage of their parents, but did not feel they were necessarily upset by the experience. At St. George's, teachers commonly attributed children's work or behaviour 'problems' to 'unstable' home life. Mr Gordon estimated that the number of single-parent families had never been higher. Teachers told how parents' meetings sometimes indicated new household arrangements. 'One mother introduced me to the girl's uncle, a boy of about seventeen, I didn't believe it'.

Mr Gordon did not distinguish between the terrace house and estate families in his view of their attitude to money. Possibly due to 'hard times' they were 'very careful', and becoming more so. School photos were not selling so well, and the specialist teacher had stopped offering the children's pottery work for a modest price because of poor parental response. By coincidence, both Greenleigh and St. George's fund raising fete was held on the same Saturday. Mr Gordon was concerned to find, through a contact, that the smaller number of Greenleigh parents had raised twice that of St. George's.

Teachers at the two schools defined and explained the characteristics of the 'children in this school' out of their own daily experiences, sometimes in contrast to experiences in other schools. As far as I am aware, only I had observed the children (and teachers) in both schools. In conventional terms, those of Greenleigh were the better behaved; quieter, more polite, tidy and less disputatious among themselves.

Two differences between the schools became clear soon after making observations at St. George's. Overheard conversation between children at St. George's were often about things other than the work they were doing, such as last night's television or playground activities.

Did you see Michael Jackson? Ain't he got a lovely voice.

You gonna play football after school? We could be in Garry's team.

The talk at Greenleigh was usually of the work in hand. Children at St. George's responded to teachers in a cheeky way rarely met at Greenleigh, often to raise a laugh with other children.

> *T:* Justin, are you eating?
> *Justin:* No!
> *T:* Why are your jaws moving?
> *J:* Chewing paper.
> *T:* Put it in the bin.

He does so, grinning at the other children.

The material conditions of the school were different. In chapter 5 I discussed how this may have had consequences for the control of children's behaviour. Mr. Gordon attributed some of the poor behaviour to the 'geography' of St. George's (Ironically, some teachers at St. George's spoke of the 'chaos' they thought open plan schools engendered. Those at Greenleigh thought so too, 'standards' would be hard to maintain, *before* they moved into the new open plan building). The schools also differed in the extent to which the children were taught in different places by different teachers, and this too had consequences for the teachers' control and possibly the children's behaviour (chapter 5). The pedagogy at Greenleigh put a premium on the children talking to one another about their work in cooperative learning, which may account for fewer non-work conversations than at St. George's.

At both schools, teachers defined families in social class terms, and attributed the characteristics of children to their families of origin. Taking into account the different material conditions and different teaching organization, the observed differences between the children of Greenleigh and St. George's may be attributed to differences in their presenting social class cultures. Whilst not using these terms, this was the substance of the explanation of the generally 'good' qualities of the children of Greenleigh, made by their teachers. The equivalent explanation of the less favourable qualities of those of St. George's was only implied by teachers.

However, it is entirely plausible to suggest that the observed (by me) and defined (by the separate sets of teachers) differences in the children's behaviour was related to the social class composition of the schools. Several studies have shown that when teachers' assessments of children's work and behaviour are analyzed by parents' occupation, the means for middle class children are higher, that is more favourable, than those of working class. (Goodacre, 1968; Brandis and Bernstein, 1976; King, 1972; Mortimore *et al*, 1987.) The third year teachers at St. George's reports on their classes effort and attainment in mathematics and English, and in 'general conduct', were on average 'better' for middle than working class children. This was so only in the top two streams, there being no identifiable middle class children in the bottom stream. The numbers involved in this exercise are too small to reach statistical significance. The teachers did not express consciousness of these differences but they were responding to their experience of children's behaviour as an aspect of their social class presenting cultures.

Boys and Girls

Teachers' inferences and definitions of the children's social origins were vague compared with the precision with which they defined boys and girls. The precision was related to biological sex differences. This was the basis of the provision of separate lavatories, but even this was really a consequence of defining the social form of sexuality, *gender*, as being different. The social meaning of being a boy or a girl differed between the two schools. At Greenleigh the metaphor of openness had informed Mr Kirby's policy of reducing differences. In registers and other documents children's names were listed alphabetically. With the exception of games, other than mixed shinty, the curriculum was undifferentiated. At traditional St. George's where some teachers referred to Mr Gordon as 'being against trendy things like women's lib and anti-sexism', boys' and girls' names were listed separately in all documents. There were no mixed games, and in the fourth year art and science were taught separately to boys and girls (chapter 4). Girls and boys, were commonly lined up, entered and exited separately, girls before boys, because 'it's convenient'. The same convenience was found in collecting and distributing things, and in dividing a class for activities. 'Girls sing first. Boys second'.

The organization of Greenleigh differentiated little between boys and girls, and nor did the teachers in their definitions of their work and behaviour (chapter 5). But at St. George's, teachers commonly defined boys as a group, as being less well behaved than girls, a generalization confirmed in their assessments (and agreed with by the children them-selves. See chapter 5). At Greenleigh there was no difference in the distribution of boys and girls in the maths sets. So too at St. George's, but girls were statistically over–represented in the top sets for English and French. The latter was recognized by teachers, and defined as being a consequence of differences in interest and even ability.

Class chances in education has been a dominant theme of the post-war sociology of education in Britain. In 1971, I drew attention to the then neglect of the different educational experiences of boys and girls. This neglect has been extensively remedied, the feminist movement having given problem-status to differences once taken for granted as natural. However, explanations of gender differences should take into account social class differences, (King, 1971; 1987).

Teachers at Greenleigh explained the children's generally favourable qualities as a consequence of their largely middle class origins. Although less clearly explicated by the teachers their reservations about the children's behaviour at St. George's could be related to the children more often coming from working class homes. However, it was the boys at St. George's who were defined as being the less well-behaved, which had led to separate science and art classes, and the end of drama classes. Third year teachers assessed boys' behaviour less favourably than that of girls, and that of working class children. Although the numbers are too small to be statistically significant, as may be expected, the least favourably assessed behaviour was that of working class boys (whose work was also the least favourably assessed). This is in accord with larger scale surveys (Brandis and Bernstein, 1974; Davie *et al*, 1972).

This suggests that gender is social class related, that being a boy or a girl varies by social origin. Child-rearing varies by both sex of child and social class, (Bronfenbrenner, 1958; Newson and Newson, 1976). In John and Elizabeth Newson's (1976) study of Nottingham families, mothers' reports of the use of smacking, threats of external authorities, and children's playing in the streets were more commonly working class, and more common for boys of all classes. Middle class children have more home-based lives, playing indoors with friends, reading and writing for their own pleasure but more often for girls of all classes. If middle class children are typically home and garden children, then some working class girls show some convergence with this life-style. Among working class children, it is the boys who are more typically street children, with less parental supervision or more autonomy than girls.

In a study of four primary schools, Clarrincoates (1978) found teachers defining and relating to children mainly on the basis of the children's presenting social characteristics, derived from the sex-stratification and class conditions of their families and localities of origin. From this it may be suggested that the teacher's definition of the poorer behaviour of boys at St. George's, is explained by the gender variant of their social class presenting culture; they were mainly working class boys.

The nature of their gender social-class specific behaviour is shown in comparisons of that observed and reported between the boys and girls at St. George's, and between the boys at St. George's and Greenleigh. At St. George's, they were in some teachers' view 'sports mad' especially football. Given the opportunity, they followed sports projects (chapter 4), decked the classroom with sports icons, and read sports magazines clandestinely in lessons. There was an extensive economy of exchange and purchase of these magazines and sports cards. Football, with large balls (banned at Greenleigh), dominated the time and space of playtime, dinner hour, before and after school in the playground. Small girls reported being intimidated by boys when they trespassed on a game-space, by having the ball kicked hard at them. Mr Gordon, the headteacher, half jokingly said the best punishment for badly behaved boys would be to take their footballs away.

One teacher did use the term 'macho' to describe boys at St. George's. At Greenleigh, 'quite a lot of boys, are well, sort of soft. We sometimes laugh and say some of the girls would make a better football team'. Football related behaviour could sometimes be seen in the classrooms of St. George's, with mock aggressive punching, elbowing and tripping, between boys and even between boys and girls (not between girls). Boys would celebrate getting their work right with hands clasped over their heads or raised clenched fist. A child, whether boy or girl, at Greenleigh, would typically look down modestly if congratulated for good work, almost embarrassed. If reproved for bad behaviour, boys at St. George's would often protest their innocence, 'It wasn't me. It was Gary Watson'. (I have no record of tale-telling at Greenleigh.)

Only the behaviour of boys was defined as being poor enough for them to be passed up the hierarchy to be punished by the headteachers at St. George's (See chapter 5). Mr Gordon reported his dealing with those who urinated in the drinking fountain for the amusement of watching other children unknowingly drink, and others who grabbed boys and split their trousers. A victim called the practice 'wedgies' where underpants were pulled hard into the crotch, 'and it don't 'arf 'urt'. Mr Gordon summarized 'if there are behaviour problems it's more a boy problem than it is a girl one. But that's not unusual, it's commonplace'. Not at Greenleigh however. He suggested that being 'inundated' with boys could explain the 'problem'. Few mixed schools have an equal number of boys and girls, and although in each year boys outnumbered girls at St. George's, they formed 52 per cent of the roll. At Greenleigh they were 53 per cent. The 'problem' of boys at St. George's was not how many there were, but what kind of boys they were — working rather than middle class.

Age and Ability

The British educational system is conspicuously age-stratified, with children changing schools and classes in age-cohorts by the arbitary school year. Internationally, children more commonly move at fixed times of the year by their level of achievement — the grade or standard system, of the USA, Eastern Bloc countries, and of Britain before the introduction of streaming. Developmental psychology was used to legitimize the view that children were best taught in age-homogeneous groups. This was made compatible within the psychometric paradigm (Esland, 1971) by calculating intelligence quotients by the ratio of measured mental age to chronological age.

Children may start at infants' school at the beginning of any three terms, often joining children already at school in mixed-age classes. Infants' teachers are very conscious of the chronological age of the children they teach, knowing most of their birthdays, which are commonly celebrated in school (King, 1978). Junior school teachers sometimes reported looking up children's dates of birth in the register, but felt they learnt very little or nothing about their ability or behaviour. 'In any case it's (age) taken into account in the (intelligence) tests'. Children were seen as part of age cohorts, first years, second years etc, and each cohort was defined differently, most clearly, the first and fourth years ('Fourth-yearitis' will be discussed in chapter 9).

First years, newly arrived from first school were to be socialized into the new work primacy, in ways described in chapter 2, with the end of play as learning and of innocence in intention. At Greenleigh, virtually all the children transferred from the adjacent 'little' school. At St. George's, they came from a number of schools, two quite commonly (the proportions varied from year to year). Children were defined by their school of origin. Those from the Langley first school were thought to have experienced a pedagogy closer to that of St. George's than those who came from the open-plan Gregory school, who were 'all over the place'. It took half a term to 'knock them into shape', 'learn our ways', whatever their school of origin or destination.

Historically, age-stratification went with ability-stratification in the

British educational system, between schools, grammar and modern, and within schools by streaming. Greenleigh was only ability-stratified through mathematics sets (although the term was not used). Teachers did not define children as being different other than in mathematical ability according to their group. St. George's was closer to historical practice, being ability stratified through more extensive setting, streaming and 'remedial' classes. Children were typified as group members mainly by their defined capacity to learn, but were considered to have other characteristics too.

The relationship between group ability-status and behaviour is well-established in the research literature, with low-status associated with teacher-defined poor behaviour (for example, Hargreaves, 1968; Barker Lunn, 1970). Explaining the relationship was not easy. Was poor behaviour a consequence of low-status, or vice-versa? Was poor behaviour the presenting culture of low school status children from predominantly low social class status families? Whatever the explanation, teachers at St. George's generally confirmed the relationship out of their own experience, reporting the poorer behaviour of low set children 'as you would expect'. Expectations were not always fulfilled. The music specialist was able to compare the third year streams, and found the middle stream better behaved than the top, 'Funny because you'd expect the less able to be more of a nuisance'. It is common in both streaming and setting, for the more able groups to be larger, a consequence of their being defined as being better behaved. This was so at St. George's. Were the middle stream better behaved because they were a smaller group? She thought not, she'd never got on with the top stream, 'they think they're rather clever'.

The third year bottom stream was sometimes referred to as the 'remedial group', not a term accepted by their teacher, who thought that she was unable to give the fourteen children the individual attention required for 'proper' remedial work. The term was also used for the first year group taught each morning for mathematics and English. The teachers of both groups associated ability with age. The children were using books and material intended to be used, on average, by younger children, and they achieved standards of average younger children. In consequence, in the third year bottom stream, 'I treat these ten and eleven year olds like seven or eight year olds'. In the first year remedial group, 'with these children you have to treat them like infants'. These children were what their teachers expected of 'the bottom end of the ability range', although that position they thought, could have been a consequence of the high proportion of them having no father at home, or being fostered or in care. That she had twice as many boys as girls in the bottom stream, did not surprise their teacher. However, the first year remedial group teacher was surprised to have more girls than boys for the first time in eight years.

Teachers' typifications of groups of children were generalizations of their experience of individual children. The typification and assessment of individual children is the subject of Chapter 7.

7 Typification and Assessment: Individual Children

All our typifications are evaluative. Like ideologies they expressed what we think is, and what we think ought to be. Teachers' control of classroom behaviour is based upon value-judgments of 'good' behaviour (chapter 5). Just as the control of behaviour is itself an assessment of behaviour, so teachers' typifications are assessments. Those of groups, 'children in this school', boys and girls, age and ability, could have real consequences for the structure of learning and teaching. Definitions of the behaviour of boys and the ability of some children, lead to single-sex and 'remedial' groups at St. George's (chapter 6).

Each teacher 'got to know' each child she taught, a process taking about half a term. 'Getting to know' lead to the construction of typifications of each child. This process was quicker and clearer when the teacher taught a child nearly all the time, as at Greenleigh, and in the first and third years of St. George's. But in the latter, setting meant that some teachers saw some children only a few times a week, and even by the Summer term, there were children who they 'didn't really know'.

It would not have been possible for me to elicit and record all the teachers' typifications of all the children, nearly a thousand in the two schools. My analysis is of the *process* of typification, drawing upon a range of data. Teachers made public their definitions of aspects of individual children in their classroom control.

Jason, finished first as usual. Wandering again, Samantha.

Sometimes, in discussing an incident the teacher would give me her thumb-nail sketch of the child involved. I asked the two third year teachers at Greenleigh to do so for each child. At my suggestion, one said these into a tape recorder, and then we taped a discussion of the transcript. The second preferred to write them, and these too we discussed. At St. George's, the three third year teachers completed a version of the end of year report, which they knew only I would see (chapter 5). With the two headteachers' permission, I had access to the children's files, including their reports. These had been written with a readership of parents and children in mind. In the spirit of openness, at Greenleigh the teachers' completed record cards served as the report to parents (chapter 2), but teachers still took them into account; 'there are some things you can't say' and 'you have to colour it a bit sometimes'.

The filed records were available to the teachers, who made little use of them. Like infants' teachers (King, 1978) they wanted to define the children out of their own experience, 'Don't want my mind made up for me'. New children arrived with substantial files of material from their first schools. A headteacher of one such school had been upset to find much of this material was thrown away (King, 1978). This disregard happened at Greenleigh and St. George's. At the former, Mr Kirby thought the information was 'subjective and sometimes emotive', 'all very general'. The marks of standardized tests were suspect, and like Mr Gordon, he put his trust in those given under his control. Mr Gordon was concerned that first school records might lead to reception class teachers defining children unfairly. He removed anything 'too personal or anything that might prejudice a teacher against a child'. He corrected the records of a boy, which were the worst 'he had even seen', but, 'he was no more trouble than any other boy (*sic*)'. They all deserved 'a new start', 'clean slate'. (In turn, the records and files were sent on to the comprehensive schools the children left for. Mr Gordon's suspicion that 'they are probably not looked at', was broadly confirmed by the liaison teacher from the comprehensive most St. George's children went on to. They too preferred to put their trust in their own tests and experiences.)

Systematic record-keeping is a bureaucratic process, standardized and formalized. In the two schools, as in all Nossex schools, the local education authority record card was kept. This included standardized test scores and comments on progress and attainment. In the spirit of openness, the card served as a report to parents at Greenleigh, but it was not the only standardized form. After his appointment Mr Kirby introduced his own.

> We needed some kind of systematic development of record keeping and I frankly had not the confidence that the staff understood what I meant by records and so I plumped for children to have a simplified record themselves.

Each child was responsible for their mathematics record sheet, reading record, including the title, author and date completed of books read outside the reading scheme (Ginn), and a science record sheet of the cards completed in the *Science from the Beginning* scheme and science experiments.

The sheets were kept in the child's tray and completed independently of the teacher, accessible to others.

> . . . it does enable the child, very quickly, to be identified by somebody coming in who doesn't know him very well, by picking up his chart.

Teachers at St. George's kept their own records of children's progress, which only they had access to (as did those of Greenleigh, supplementary to the standardized system). The report form at St. George's had been designed by Mr Gordon. This provided spaces for mathematics, English, 'general subjects' and behaviour reports, which were detailed by teachers in different ways. Thus mathematics often was sub-headed 'Tables' and English, with spelling, handwriting and 'creative'. General subjects sometimes included topic work, folders, art, physical education and games. Whatever the headings the assessment was for 'attainment' and 'effort', only mathematics reports used percentages. Attainment and effort were coded, A very good, B good, C average, D below average and E weak. Those for attainment were distributed in a 'normal' way, with roughly five per cent A's. Mr Gordon wanted to have a 'national standard'. In consequence, only top set children were given A's for attainment.

The Typification and Assessment Process

Infants' teachers typify and assess children in terms of their being unique developing personalities (King, 1978) whose nature may have consequences for a child's learning progress. The primacy of work in the junior teachers' ideology puts *learning progress* at the centre of the typification and assessment process. Their talk of a child is mainly about how well they are getting on with their work. The 'yardstick' they used in their judgments was the child's ability, a measure of which, scores on standardized tests, were part of their consciousness (chapter 2). These were not the totality of the child, 'I don't think that's IQ 116 over there' but the basic explanation of their progress.

> A great improvement (in reading) but not up to the standard of his age.

> Neil always works to the best of his ability.

Whatever validity and reliability of standardized tests, they are probably the best *single* predictor of achievement. The correlation with verbal-reasoning scores are all statistically significant for the third years for both schools. At Greenleigh those with reading book and Fletcher book were based on assessments largely independent of the individual teachers and so can be for the whole year group without committing an aggregative fallacy (King, 1980). Those for the three streams at St. George's are based on the teachers' ratings of attainment, and so reported separately in table 3 below.

The social significance, for the teachers, of the use of standardized ability tests was to show what the child had achieved in relation to his or her imputed potential. Such definitions could be made explicit to parents, as in this incident at Greenleigh.

> A mother had 'phoned the headteacher, complaining that her son's reading book is 'too easy' for him. Mr Kirby checks his reading age in the file and which book he is on from the reading record in his tray. He 'phones the mother back. Her son has a reading age of 6.3 and is therefore on the 'correct' book.

Although children could have similar achievements, the significance for the teacher could be different.

> Sadie, she's had two IQs up in the 112's something like that. When you put that against Kerry, who might be 94 or 95, you look at their work, there's really not an awful lot of difference between them. I don't think she's doing as well as she could do.

Measured ability was not the only index of potential. A child's highest level of achievement was also used.

> Kevin is the cleverest boy in the class but has no stars for good work. His teacher knows he is capable, by the quality of work he sometimes produces, and he should be up to doing it again.

> Is that all you've done since yesterday? (Shows small gap between finger and thumb). You get two stars for work and now this.

Teachers' typifications of children incorporated explanations of why their

Table 3: Product-moment correlations with verbal-reasoning scores

Greenleigh n=54	Fletcher 0.54	Reading 0.61
St. George's	*Mathematic attainment*	*English attainment*
Top stream n=35	0.62	0.54
Middle stream n=24	0.67	0.72
Bottom stream n=14	0.62	0.59

(All correlations statistically significant at least 5 per cent level by t test.)

work progress was sometimes below their 'ability'. From the data found and created the different elements in the process were quite clear; learning capacity, friendships, behaviour in school, state of health, home and family. I examined all my sources, and collated all the examples of two or more elements occurring together. The relationships between them can be summarized as follows:

> A child's learning progress depends upon his or her learning capacity. Progress may be affected by the child's state of health. It may also be affected by home and family conditions, friends and behaviour in school, each of which may influence the others.

The structure of the typification process is shown in the following figure:

Figure 1   Teachers' typifications of individual children

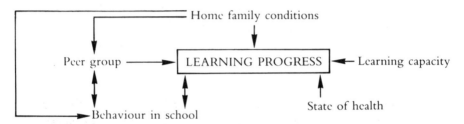

In typifying 'children in this school', teachers collated and generalized their typifications of individual children (chapter 6). Just as the characteristics of children were related to their collective family/home conditions, so were those of individuals to their particular conditions. The curriculum and pedagogy of junior school practices provides teachers with their data as described in chapter 6.

A child's family/home background was defined as having both favourable and unfavourable consequences for learning progress.

> Daniel is good at oral work. He obviously converses a great deal with grown ups at home, and seems to have a good relationship with his real dad, who's left the home, and his mother's second husband.

> Tracey's father is a lorry driver, often away. Her mother works. She is a 'latch key' child who spends time with her granny in another part of the town. They enjoy one another's company. Their own Darby and Joan Club. Tracey's absences are suspected to be extended visits to her granny. A nice girl, but her work suffers. (Teachers' oral accounts.)

Family/home background could be defined as the source of behaviour 'problems'.

> Simon's poor behaviour today is due to his visiting his divorced mother over the weekend; she has a new boy friend. Can't expect them to leave their family problems at home. Can't forget them entirely at school.

Teachers would seek information about a child's home to explain a problem.

> Sometimes I search it out if there's a problem. I will ask, say, how did Timothy strike you last year? Two former teachers say mum and dad have (too) high expectations.

> Two teachers discuss Jonathan, who is 'struggling' in his group for maths. Should he be moved? Not yet. All the family involved in amateur theatre productions. 'May have something to do with it'.

> Mark's a bright boy, but very difficult to motivate at times. Seems almost comatose. I'll ask his mother if he gets sufficient sleep.

Illness, resulting in absence from school, could be defined as retarding learning progress. The real consequence was usually to create more time to catch up with lost work, especially the important mathematics, at the expense of other subjects or through extra homework.

Children are not responsible for their family, home backgrounds or their sometimes being unwell, but with the end of innocence they were given responsibility for their behaviour in schools (chapter 2 and 5), and this could be defined as having an effect on their learning progress.

> Tracy — a chatterer, inclined to be fussy and too interested in things going on in the classroom and so a certain amount of carelessness in her work.

Not only could poor behaviour lead to poor work but difficulties with work could be defined as a cause for poor behaviour. 'Tends to chat when written work becomes difficult'. At St. George's, teachers' assessments of children's achievements in English and mathematics were positively correlated with those for good behaviour (see table 4). The correlations are not only statistically significant, but in Weber's (1948) terms, significant 'at the level of meaning'. They are quantifications of the teachers' constructs. Their typifications pose a casual correlation between children's

Table 4: Product-moment correlations with teacher's assessments of behaviour, St. George's

Stream (n=)	Attainments: Mathematics	English
Top (35)	0.49	0.73
Middle (24)	0.69	0.69
Bottom (14)	0.63	0.66

(All correlations statistically significant to at least the 5 per cent level by t test.)

work and behaviour. 'At the level of meaning' the direction of causality is not fixed; the quality of behaviour may affect the quality of work and vice versa.

The peer group relations of infants are an important part of their teachers' typifications, not only as an indication of their adaptation to school but also their social development. In the juniors, friendships, like play, are the province of children, and of less interest to their teachers. Only rarely would a teacher intervene for 'social' reasons. Most of the Greenleigh children had transferred from the adjacent first school, but Nicholas had come from a private school. Mrs Mackenzie asked Jonathan to 'look after him', and help him make friends. Teachers' interest in children's peer groups was in their consequences for their work progress.

> Sadie is very friendly with Kerry and seems to live in her shadow all the time. She could do much better work, she is more able than Kerry but doesn't seem to bother, she coasts along just enough to get by and works down to Kerry's standard which is rather a pity.

Friends were defined as influencing behaviour and so work.

> I am sure Richard could do better if he put his mind to it, but he seems to enjoy being the centre of attention by being disruptive in the class.

Teachers' typifications of individual children were definitions of what was 'real' about the children. To paraphrase W.I. Thomas (1926), 'If people define situations as real, they are real in their consequences'. What were the real consequences of teachers' definitions of children? Defining children's learning progress in terms of their 'ability' had no direct consequence since the quality was relatively fixed and 'they can do nothing about it'. (Definitions of ability did have real consequences for which group children were assigned to, chapter 2 and 3.) Teachers could do little about a child's state of health or home, family conditions, except sometimes to make suggestions to parents about things like bedtime and helping with reading. Although teachers did little about who was friends with who, they did intervene in peer group structures to the extent of controlling who worked or sat next to who, when this affected work and behaviour (chapter 5).

Typifications and assessments served several purposes for the teachers. Test and records could be used to show parents what their child had achieved against what imputed potential. The authority of standardized tests is not easily challenged. The process also provides teachers with some estimate of their own effectiveness in helping children achieve to their imputed potential, and indicates what may be done to narrow the gap between potential and fulfilment. In most cases it was to raise the latter to the former. Although some children were doing as well as their ability allowed, none were defined as doing better, thereby confirming the definition of their ability.

Children's Typifications of Learning Progress

We all make sense of social situations through the process of typification, and children are no exceptions. At school, they typify groups of children in the same dimensions as their teachers; children in this school, children in my class, boys, girls, first year, second etc and by ability, top group etc. Individual children are typified largely in terms of friendship relations. These are very much the concern of sociometric studies (Blyth, 1960), but more recently more qualitative methods have been used. Sluckin (1981), following the tradition of the folklorists Iona and Peter Opie (1958; 1969), made direct observations in playgrounds, speaking his observations into a tape recorder to the interest and amusement of the children. Davies (1982) and Pollard (1985) used interviews, the latter engaging the children to interview one another.

It was not part of my research purpose to make a study of children's peer groups. My interest was in understanding how they defined or typified learning progress; the important business of school work (chapter 2). Each child typified his or herself and most others in their teaching group. As with teachers' typifications, my interest was not in the individual examples, many hundreds in potential, but the process of making sense of learning progress.

My sources were varied; the interviews with children, overheards in school and playground, the third year questionnaire and follow-up discussions (chapter 1). The collation of this found and created data showed the same elements accounting for learning progress as were used by their teachers; learning capacity, friendships, behaviour in school, state of health, home and family background. An analysis showed them to be related in the following way:

> How well you do at school depends on how clever you are, but may be affected by your family and by illness. It is also affected by your friends and how well you behave, and these can each affect the other.

Children were well-aware of how well they and their classmates were doing in their work. At St. George's teachers' assessments were made public in reading out test and homework marks, and by lists on notice boards. Although the children of Greenleigh kept their own record sheets, who was on which Fletcher or reading book and which science card was well-known. School reports, although addressed to parents, were known to children. 'I hate reports because my dad wants me to be good at everything'. Apart from this bureaucratized assessment, all pedagogical practices are imbued with signals of assessment as teachers publicly praise and criticize children's work. At St. George's, the award of House points was the emblemic ritualization of success. 'Good' work was displayed at Greenleigh, with significance as to where. In the corridor was better than in the classroom, but best was in the entrance hall.

The third years of St. George's were asked to tick the names of children in their class who were 'good at school work' and were invited to 'tick yourself if you want to'. Each child could be assigned work status by the number of peers grading them 'good'. In each class these were positively and significantly correlated with their teachers' assessments of their English and mathematics attainments. At Greenleigh, the children were asked to tick their classmates (and themselves) if they were generally 'quick to finish their work', and 'good or fairly good at mathematics'. (The children were generally modest in the expression of how well they were doing. Even those who acknowledged and were acknowledged by others to be well-ahead in mathematics, only admitted to be 'Fairly good', hence the phrase used.) The children's mathematics status was positively and significantly correlated with their position in the Fletcher Scheme (table 5). This analysis does not show that individual children necessarily agreed with their teachers' assessment of their work but that the collectivity of children did so.

Like their teachers, the children defined differences in learning progress in terms of differences in learning capacity. Although by making the scores available to their parents, the children of Greenleigh's may have had access to their verbal reasoning quotients, none in either school spoke of IQ or reading age. Learning capacity was expressed in terms

Table 5: *Product-moment correlations of peer work-status and achievement*

St. George's	Good at school work	
	Mathematics achievement	*English achievement*
Top stream (n=35)	0.62	0.54
Middle (n=24)	0.62	0.68
Bottom (n=14)	0.70	0.67
Greenleigh	Good or fairly good at mathematics/ position in Fletcher Scheme	
Mixed ability group I (n=27)	0.68	
Mixed ability group II (n=27)	0.72	

(All correlations statistically significant to at least the 5 per cent by t test.)

of being 'brainy', 'clever', and occasionally, 'intelligent'. Asked why some are more clever than others, the usual reply was 'they just are'; a natural and immutable endowment.

> *RK:* Will the slow ones (at work) ever catch up with the quick ones?
> *Girl:* No. Some are still on the books I did in the baby's (school).

Like their teachers, children had a concept of a standard of work for their age, and individuals who fell well below it were judged immature.

> *T:* Is that all you've done?
> *Boy:* He's too busy cuddling his teddy bear.

The consequences of general behaviour in school for work progress were well-recognized. Those doing well were sometimes described by others as 'goody-goodies'. Those doing less well were 'show-offs' who 'mucked about'. This relationship could be admitted. A boy who had been demoted for maths explained he had mucked about because he found the work 'boring', but was pleased to have easier work to do in the lower set. I asked a group whether they decide to 'behave themselves' or not. A girl, who thought herself well-behaved, said of those not so, 'Sometimes they try (to behave), but it's a bit like a habit of smoking, after you start you want to stop but you can't stop yourself doing it'. All the correlations between children's assessments of work and behaviour were statistically significant; poor work and behaviour went together (table 6).

Children could define the relationship between, behaviour and work progress as a consequence of learning capacity (as could teachers).

People that are average, that are not very good at school work,

Table 6: *Product-moment correlations of children's work and behaviour status*

St. George's	Top Stream (n=35)	Middle (n=24)	Bottom (n=14)
	−0.49	−0.64	−0.66
Greenleigh	Mixed-ability Group I (n=27)	Group II (n=27)	
Good or quite good at mathematics	−0.54	−0.59	
Quick to finish work	−0.57	−0.50	

(All correlations statistically significant to at least the 5 per cent level by t test. For interpretation purposes the sign of the correlations should be reversed.)

just muck about and don't listen enough. The brainy ones act sensible and just listen.

Individual children could attribute slowing of their work progress to illness, largely through absence from school, and, like their teachers, accepted the importance of catching up, especially in mathematics. In this they might engage the help of their parents. In general, the influence of home and family on work progress was thought to be through specific help with reading, preparing for tests and collecting project material. The imputed help of other children's parents could be thought unfair.

We've got a girl in our (mathematics) group; when she finishes her work at home she gets it all right, but not here.

Children were not necessarily appreciative of their parents' interest.

When I get my homework and my mum fusses about it, you've gotta do it now, you've gotta do it tonight, when I say I do it tomorrow. (A boy, on what he didn't like about school.)

Homework could be preferable to domestic chores.

If you haven't got homework you've got to help you mum do the dishes and all that. (A girl, on what she did like about school.)

The only specific type of family defined by children was those of teachers, whose children were sometimes thought to be at an unfair advantage in 'coming from a brainy family'.

When children typified other children, they did so principally in terms of friendship. Sociometric studies show that children make friends with those who they come into contact with most often and who they define as being rather like themselves (Blyth, 1960). Third years were asked to tick the names of children in their class who were their friends, and were asked to write the names of other friends in the school. In every case the majority of friends were in their class, and with them most of the time. The number of friendship choices received was an index of popularity or informal status. Most choices were of children of the same sex, so that each class had at least two informal status systems, one for each sex. The correlation between the number of friendship choices made by boys and those made by girls, were all significant and negative (see table 7).

The questionnaire asked children to assess their own and their classmates' behaviour and work, and to name who their friends were. An analysis of the assessments and choices of individual children, showed that the majority of friends named by most children were subjectively defined as being as good at work and as well behaved, as the individual concerned. Children choose as friends those who they define as being rather like themselves. Friendships would sometimes be defined as having favourable consequences for learning. 'Now I'm with people I like, I work better'. The poor behaviour of other children could be attributed to their peer group relations. 'He just mucks about to show off to his friends'.

Table 7:   Rank-order correlations, number of friendship choices of boys and girls

St. George's		Greenleigh	
Top stream (35) −0.75		Mixed-ability group I (27) −0.78	
Middle (24) −0.64		II (27) −0.78	
Bottom (14) −0.68			

(All correlations statistically significant to at least the 5 per cent level by t test).

Children spend much of their waking time at school. At Greenleigh and St. George's, most enjoyed the experience of conforming and being controlled to standards of behaviour they found acceptable, in relation to work they thought important, in the company of their friends. Although individual children's typifications of their work progress may not necessarily have accorded with that of their teacher, there was a correspondence in the process of typification both used. Both drew upon the shared daily experience of classroom activity.

8   The Teachers

I have described what I observed teachers doing, and have tried to explain why they did what they did in terms of their recipe ideology of a particular kind of child-centered education. Ideologies provide an over-arching conception of experience which becomes part of the way those who hold the ideology conceive themselves, that is, their *social identities*. This attempt to understand what it is to be a teacher of juniors draws upon teachers' comments and accounts of their work. Teachers' experience and identities showed some variation between the two schools, differences which were to a degree consequences of the particular ideologies and identities of the *headteachers*. I also give an account of two sets of teachers, the first of which showed some convergence with infants' teachers, the second a different divergence from the junior teacher norm.

Professional Identity and Interests

The characteristic manner of infants' teachers in relating to children was marked by what I called professional pleasantness, affection and equanimity, (King, 1978). That of juniors did show a measure of the first, some of the second, but little of the third. Unlike infants' teachers they sometimes exhibited professional crossness.

Unlike infants' teachers, those of juniors do not define the children's being happy as a pre-requisite of successful learning, but a bonus. Providing that work was accomplished, teachers' manner was often that of *professional pleasantness* neither false nor forced, but brisk and businesslike, part of being the teacher. It could be used with individual children, groups or the whole class. Compared with infants' teachers, the faces would be less bright and smiling, the eyes less stretched open wide, with rather less eye-contact. They stood up straight, feet together, hands behind back, speaking carefully, stressing the important words. Humour was part of their pleasantness (sarcasm and irony were rare) (chapter 5) *Professional affection*, was an extension of this pleasantness, shown in the use of endearments, 'my love', 'little one' and 'dear', but did not extend to the degree of physical contact found with infants; little more than a pat on the head, and no holding of hands on playground duty. The thought of sitting a child on their laps amused them, especially as some of the older ones were bigger than some teachers.

The professional equanimity of infants' teachers was based upon presumptions of children's innocence; that they hadn't intended to knock the paints over four times or let the hamster out, and so should not be directly rebuked. Juniors are defined as knowing they are being naughty and sometimes choosing to be so (chapter 2). *Professional crossness* was the teacher's expression of enough is enough. It was not loss of temper, but 'acting up a bit', 'turning it on'. With experience, I felt I could predict when a performance was likely to occur. Some children felt they could too, looking at the teacher, shsshing the others and making warning touches with their hands. If the pre-emptive action were successful, a sigh of relief was sometimes audible, even made by the teacher, with an acknowledging nod of the head and screwed up eyes. Naughtiness had been acknowledged by all concerned; the end of innocence. Children did complain to me of their teacher being 'in a mood', but most reported enjoying school (chapter 2). Most teachers appeared to like most of the children they taught; none expressed dislike of even those defined as the 'biggest nuisances'.

Teachers' satisfaction was centred on helping children achieve standards of work as high as their individual, imputed capacities allowed; a process thought to have been completed by the final year. The infant-first school was regarded as a not too effective preparation for this. The comprehensive school could fail to build on the developed potential.

> A comprehensive school has sent the O-level results of former pupils. Staffroom comments are generally that children have done less well than expected. 'Should have got an A grade in English and mathematics!'

Their explanation was that the children had been taught by too many teachers; a product of 'artificial subject specialism'. Another consequence was that the comprehensives had pastoral care systems to deal with children's problems. It was a matter of pride that such provision was considered unnecessary in junior schools. The relative absence of 'problems' and the successful realization of potential were mainly attributed to the quality of child-teacher relationships, founded on the *class-teacher*.

Compulsory elementary education in the nineteenth century led to larger schools and the grouping of children by the architecture of the cellular or egg-crate model (Lortie, 1975). The decline of the pupil-teacher system led to the norm of one teacher per classroom, the class-teacher who taught the children all or most of the time. This was virtually so at Greenleigh, but there had been a time when a form of team or cooperative teaching had been used, thought by the headteacher to be appropriate to the open plan. Teachers were pleased it was discontinued. The 'floating' teachers withdrew groups of children from larger units to work in the bays, but the unit teachers 'thought the children were theirs' and disliked losing them, 'tried to hang on to them'.

Being the single classteacher was liked for its flexibility, 'freedom from the timetable, follow-up things, complete things without sending them off to somebody else'. The school timetable did constrain teachers in their use of time and space, particularly access to the hall for physical education and drama, and in their use of the television, mobile on wheels. Classteachers evolved their own timetables, not always on display, and not well-known to the children, who often must not know what they were to do next, when I asked. Sometimes this was because their teacher didn't know either, there being scope for adventitious teaching, as when a discussion of 'what's in the news' included the phasing out of the half-penny, which lead to an extended question and answer mental arithmetic session. 'How many ha'pennies in seventy five pence? How many in two pounds?'

Classteachers had their own classrooms. Unlike those of infants' teachers, they were not much personalized, not made 'homely' by the introduction of furniture and curtains from home. They were for working in. They were however respected as teachers' private spaces. Colleagues and children from other classes would knock on the door or wait to receive a signal before entering. Even in doorless Greenleigh, visitors usually knocked on the entrance frame. Teachers were put out when parents came straight in, 'I looked up and there she was by my table!' The headteachers made direct entrances; they were their schools.

At St.George's, the more extensive use of setting in the second and fourth years limited class teaching. This had consequences in the children's behaviour as they moved between lessons, partly due to the teacher not knowing who was responsible, 'whose children they were' (chapter 5), Class-teachers felt responsible for 'my children' wherever they were, rebuking them for poor behaviour outside the classroom. Whilst teachers admitted the advantage of setting (chapter 3), they regretted the disadvantages. 'You can't make connections, you can't talk about something you did in the morning, when most of them weren't there'.

Ability grouping by setting (but not streaming) eroded single class teaching, as did teacher specialization. Teachers did feel they were to a degree specialized in the teaching of children of a particular age–range, 'lower' and 'upper school', but this did not necessarily prevent their teaching 'their' children all or most of the time, but *teaching subject specialization* did. Musical skills have been a relatively scarce and valued commodity among primary school teachers for some time. Although the admitted 'non–musicians' used tapes and television for their music lessons, at St. George's the two teacher–pianists took others' classes for music, and were called the music specialists. One who was 'not happy beyond book two' took no mathematics: whilst colleagues took this with her class, she took others' for music. The teaching of French in primary schools is in relative decline, but teachers who had been on special courses could be regarded as specialists (chapter 4). This was so at Greenleigh where specialist teaching led to more specialist teaching and less single class teaching. Whilst the French specialist took the fourth year, the fourth year teacher took her first year class for science or her first year colleague took them for geography. When her colleague took her class for geography, the fourth year teacher took her class for Science. Specialist teaching is incipient of more specialist teaching, and of more bureaucratic control of time and space through the timetable.

Teachers tend to maintain what Hargreaves (1967) called 'the myth of equal competence' about themselves; a form of colleague loyalty practiced at St. George's and Greenleigh. Assumed equal competence did not go with equal rewards. Like most non–manual careers, the national system of teachers' salaries is age–incremental, but further differentiated. Concern about the shortage of science and mathematics teachers in secondary schools led to the system of salary allowances for posts of 'special responsibility' in 1945. The teachers' unions, especially the National Union of Teachers with a majority of primary teachers members, have resisted all proposals to confine differentiated salary scales to one sector of the maintained school system. The system of scale post, which obtained at the time of the research, distributed such posts according to the unit total system, whereby schools had posts according to size and the age of pupils. In national terms, Greenleigh and St. George's were small and had lowly costed younger children, and so had only two and three (respectively) Scale 2 posts. The larger junior–middle schools of Newbridge did have some Scale 3s.

The distribution of scale posts within secondary schools is fairly clearly related to two forms of teacher specialization, subject specialization and administration, often in relation to pastoral care (King, 1982), both abjured in primary schools. Headteachers are always involved in the distribution of the available scale posts in a school. The legal authority of headteachers of maintained schools is in Weber's (1968) terms, *bureaucratic*, but they also exercise an historically older form of authority, *traditional authority*. One particular form of traditional authority Weber called *patrimony*, where the holder has 'free arbitariness and favour'. Without using these terms, both headteachers defined the award of scale posts this way.

Nationally, the criteria used to distribute scale posts in primary schools are not at all clear (Wallace, 1986). Headteachers often have scale post holders not of their own creation. At Greenleigh one and at St. George's two posts had been given by the current headteacher's predecessor, and both had some difficulty in discovering their basis. That held by the 'music specialist' at St. George's seemed clear enough. A second seemed to have been awarded, as Mr Gordon, in an oblique reference to the parable of the talents, put it, as the reward 'for a good and faithful servant'. This was thought to be the traditional way to a scale post, but both heads thought this was changed or changing, Mr Gordon's third scale post was awarded for special responsibility for mathematics. His proposal had to be agreed by a local authority adviser. His candidate was well-qualified in the subject, and although he would not claim she led her colleagues in their teaching of the subject, they did consult her. She remained a class teacher although teaching 'her subject' to children other than her own. She had written an outline syllabus which her new and temporary colleagues said they found useful.

One scale post at Greenleigh had apparently been awarded by Mr Kirby's predecessor on the 'good and faithful servant' basis, but he gave it precision with the title and duties of lower school leader (the first two years). A music specialist received the second scale post but, since her leaving for another school, Mr Kirby had left the scale post unused. All the posts were used at St. George's and so there was less interest in the prospect of obtaining one than at Greenleigh. However, all teachers had ideas about how the posts were obtained. The commonest idea was 'you have to be a specialist'.

Except in the case of music posts, 'specialist' did not mean specialist subject teaching. Most teachers referred to themselves and sometimes colleagues having 'strengths' and 'specialist interests', (occasionally to 'weaknesses' and things they were 'not too keen on'), and these strengths or interests were sometimes called 'specialisms'. When a teacher said she was 'not an English specialist', she meant it was not one of her favourite things to teach. They also see different teachers' 'specialisms' complementing one another in the children's overall experience. One who had done no poetry that session knew that it was a particular interest of the children's previous teacher, and so 'they've had a fair amount already'.

It was the demonstration of this kind of specialism, compatible with the model of the class-teacher, that was being suggested. How was the demonstration made? 'You have to know all the jargon, know all the rights things to say'. Saying the right things may be extended to writing the right things. Having been on a computer appreciation course it might be worth mounting a display in a public area of the school. 'Let them (*sic*) know what you've been up to'. This might be extended to making (with the headteacher's agreement) a written contribution to the collection of teachers' guidelines; a requirement for those who already had a scale post.

Permanent, long-serving teachers on scale one were sometimes discontented with blocked career mobility. 'There was a pleasant working atmosphere amongst the staff — graded posts seem to have destroyed this'. They felt undervalued, denied promotion because, 'He's (the headteacher) got us already'. Both headteachers were aware of what Mr Gordon called 'the sort of slight tension' about scale posts. He felt this could inhibit initiative and responsibility. 'It's not a case of I'm not going to do it, but without pay I don't think I've got the weight (status) to do it'. Since the leaving of the scale 2 music specialist at Greenleigh, the school orchestra had virtually lapsed and there had been no muscial productions, even though the staff included activists in local productions.

At Greenleigh, Mr Kirby was 'sitting on a scale 2 post at the moment'. 'I am looking for someone to show some clear signs of initiative and of leadership'. He saw these qualities in one of the recent appointments. 'They seem to turn to her and she has some expertise in certain directions'. He knew such a promotion would upset some longer serving staff, and although 'I'm not in the business of trying to make people's lives a misery . . . the children deserve the best we can give' even if 'they are giving (them) what they think is being an effective education'. He had produced as written 'detailed brief' for 'those members of staff wishing to take up posts of responsibility', consisting of eight paragraphs with the headings, policy, information/ideas, in-service education, classroom practice and organization, materials for designated work area, setting targets and monitoring progress continuity, and liaison. Only one candidate was meeting his specification.

It could be that times have changed but in the infants-first schools of my earlier research (King, 1978), there were no staff discontents of this kind, even though some teachers were on scale 3. Junior-middle schoolteachers, like those infants-first schools, were generally confident of their doing the best they could for the children they taught, but unlike those of the younger children were discontented by this sometimes not being acknowledged.

Variations in Professional Identities

The Teachers

The characteristic manner or style of junior school teachers was different to that of infants, but two variations were found. At St. George's two groups of children were known as 'remedial'. Their teachers referred to their having to deal with the children 'like infants'. This applied to the children's standard of work and the materials they used (chapter 6), but also to the manner of their relating to and controlling the children; they acted rather like infants' teachers. They used a greal deal of praise for the children's work 'to encourage them', despite their low levels of achievement. They also showed *professional equanimity*, never professional crossness. They either ignored or used oblique control with misbehaviour, because 'they don't really mean it', 'they can't help it'. They were attributing childhood innocence.

> David's being rude again. Says he's got ten fingers here (holds up hands), and one here (points to trousers). Teacher pretends not to hear.

Their colleagues admired their patience with the children. 'I don't know how they put up with it'.

Junior-trained teachers, teaching in infants schools retained many of the typical characteristics of junior school teachers (chapter 2 and King, 1978). Mrs Clement had been trained and had taught as an infants' teacher, but faced with redeployment, chose to move to a junior-middle school. There was little in her manner to show her infants' background, her room was the clue. She had made it hers, with an armchair brought from home for her use at reading and discussion times, and with other personal items. The room was decked more than any other with mounted displays of the children's work, some hanging from the ceiling and light fittings, just like a typical infants' classroom; She had otherwise consciously modified her style. She did not want to treat the children as 'babies' or to be thought 'babyish' in treating them so by her colleagues. She was as direct in her control methods and as insistent on the primacy of work as any colleague. She found she could modify her style quite easily by treating the children 'more like adults'. She had made an ideological shift, and changed professional identity.

Teachers, both of infants and juniors, typically tried to do their best for the children they teach; they typically showed high commitment in their child–centredness. Two teachers showed low commitment. They were different to their colleagues in a number of ways. They acknowledged the differences, which were obliquely recognized by others.

The children they taught were in conventional terms less well-behaved than others. Behaviour that would have been corrected or punished by other teachers was ignored. They never showed professional crossness. Their general manner was that of what the late Erving Goffman (1961) called role-distance; that what was going on was not a great concern to them. They used little eye scanning. (The children did not look at them when they were being naughty; they knew their gaze would not be reciprocated.) They used little of either approval or disapproval.

Both, without prompting, referred to their being different to other teachers, knowing I'd observed in their's and colleagues' classrooms. One spoke of not being 'fussed' about things like the children's 'appearance, tidyness and where they keep their things'. Other teachers did, but it was 'regimentation'. A colleague's class was referred to 'where you can hear a pin drop', 'there's no point in that'. The other spoke of having been 'in trouble with parents for not setting homework', and evenly expressed a disposition of, 'why should I split a gut pushing them to work and behave themselves? If they don't want to, why should I make them?'. These teachers showed low commitment to the child–centred ideology of junior teachers, with its primacy of school work and concomitant good behaviour. Colleagues loyalty may have limited comments from other teachers about these two (I never asked for such comments). However, one was called 'rather lax', and there were occasions when their classes' behaviour was witnessed disapprovingly by other teachers.

The origins of their ideological dissent, the basis of their differentness, was not clear. Both were mature entrants to teaching, but others who had previous adult careers were just as committed as the majority who had only worked as teachers.

The Headteachers

In England and Wales each maintained school headteacher has legal authority, *bureaucratic authority*, to organize a number of children and teachers, for a certain period of time, in buildings and with money and other resources provided by the local authority. Each is relatively fixed, although a headteacher can try to increase these resources and protect against decreases.

St George's was the only junior-middle school in Newbridge not to have an associated infants-first school. The possibility of its being turned into a combined school for five to twelve year olds had been mooted soon after reorganization but never fulfilled. Mr Gordon's predecessor was soon faced with the problem that was to occupy much of his time, recruiting pupils. 'I don't have time to do much else'. Local authority officials resisted his suggestion that they circulate all first schools, first school departments of combined schools with details and application forms for all middle schools and middle school departments, even after the 1980 Education Act giving parents such a choice. He created his own material and application form, relying on individual parents to make contact. The original plan was for St George's to have an estimated roll of 320. This target had been consistently approached, despite a fall in the primary school population in Newbridge, as nationally.

Mr. Gordon made an appointment with every interested parent showing them selected parts of the school, and particularly a first year class adjacent to his room. Why had parents chosen St George's? Mr Gordon thought that those from the nearby terraced houses were often choosing for their children to go to the school they had (chapter 6). Two first schools in Newbridge had no associated middle school. One of them was open plan with a reputation for 'progressive' methods. Children came from this school because, thought Mr Gordon, parents were dissatisfied with their progress and wanted them to have a 'traditional' education at middle school. Parental dissatisfaction with the first school departments of combined schools, was the motive he thought led to their choosing not to send their children into the middle school department, but to St George's.

> I have had people say to me, well they are struggling at So and So first school. They don't say the child isn't very bright, they say they are not doing very well which is the school's fault of course — they will be better in a different school.

Part of the attraction of St George's to parents of 'struggling' children was the remedial provision.

> As soon as you do that of course you make a rod for your own back, and that attracts more, people talk amongst themselves, ah well they have got a special teacher at St George's so more come

because of that. Which means you don't solve the problem you create a bigger one.

The longer serving teachers agreed with his analysis and associated it with the decline they felt in the standards of behaviour (chapter 6). The four temporary teachers were grateful to have jobs teaching any sort of child. In the general condition of falling rolls, the local authority ('the County' in Mr Gordon's terms) would not create more permanent appointments; they sometimes had such posts for redeployment. Mr Gordon had each July to demonstrate the adequacy of his recruitment for the next September to justify the renewal of the temporary contracts for another year. The temporary teachers never felt 'settled'. Their careers had followed the typical sequence of supply teaching, temporary part-time and then temporary full-time appointment. One had been at St George's on this last basis for four years. At the end of my time there, Mr Gordon was successful in having three made permanent, to their evident relief and joy.

The attraction of St George's for local parents, in the view of the headteacher and some teachers, was their traditional or old-fashioned educational methods. 'They want their children to receive the kind of education they had themselves'. Was this meeting of parental choice an adaptation to attract numbers or a fortunate coincidence? The latter, thought Mr Gordon, 'I've always been in fairly formal, traditional schools'. Their pedagogy was even a school tradition, 'my predecessor — he was even more old-fashioned than I am I suppose'. The temporary teachers, pleased to have any job, were generally content to follow traditional ways, as were the permanent staff. The teachers' general commitment was shown in three of them having had their own children at the school (some time ago) and one currently.

Mr Gordon's preoccupation with recruiting pupils and retaining teachers, left him little time to teach. He took some swimming in season, helped with games, and some lessons with the bottom third year stream, so that their class teacher could take games with another year group. (Able-bodied, younger teachers could be at a premium for taking games in some schools; worth a scale post.) He knew little about the teaching of his teachers, several times saying he envied my being able to observe them at work. Most teachers confirmed their classrooms as a private space by covering the glazed door and windows with children's work and posters. Mr Gordon would enter with notices and messages sometimes glimpsing teachers' spelling mistakes on the board. Showing parents around gave him the chance to look at the children's work books and to ask them questions.

In law, it is the local authority who is responsible for the curriculum of maintained schools, but it is usual for primary headteachers to be active in its connection. Not so, Mr Gordon. By defining the curriculum and pedagogy as 'traditional' he could assume that they were in no need of formal definition or control. Everyone knows what traditional means. The appointment of a new deputy headteacher slightly changed things.

Deputy headteachers are on a separate, higher salary scale to other teachers, their position based on years of service, size of school and age of pupils (as are those of headteachers). Deputy headteachers of primary schools are almost always class teachers. They used to be appointed on the basis of long service; Mr Gordon's 'good and faithful servant' reward. This was so for the recently retired deputy headteacher. In recent times, such appointments have come to be used as 'promotion posts' for aspiring headteachers. The duties of deputy headteacher in any kind of school, are highly variable (Todd and Dennison, 1978). A visiting American student asked in the staff room, 'What do deputy headteachers do?'. The reply was hoots of laughter, and, 'you may well ask'. A reasonable answer would have been, 'What the headteacher says'.

The new deputy head was given responsibility for geography and history (sometimes he said 'humanities') but apart from this specification he, after a term, was still finding out what the job involved. When a teacher asked him for some exercise books he realized he was in charge of stationery, like his predecessor. His headteacher confirmed that he had made no job specification and was prepared for his deputy to make his own initiatives. This he did with a suggestion that the head, with a little hesitation, supported. In looking at the geography and history teaching in the school, the new deputy found no syllabus and no record of what had been taught. Investigations showed that the Romans had been taught twice in successive years, and sometimes after the Vikings. His response was to introduce a new set of textbooks, and the suggestion that the headteacher endorsed that teachers should submit a monthly report, to the head, on their curriculum activities.

Teaching plans and reports are fairly common in primary schools, but Mr Gordon had doubts about the worth of either. However, he could see the muddle that the present system was in, hence his reserved support of monthly reports. Some teachers saw a vague, sinister motive in this. They'd had no feedback from Mr Gordon on the reports they'd submitted (he'd not yet read the most recent ones, now a month old). What were they for? If they were to avoid duplication and repetition of learning, and to create better sequences of learning, when could they be consulted? Their questions were unanswered at the time I finished my visiting.

I have suggested that headteachers' authority contains an element of a form of traditional authority, which Weber (1968) called *patrimony*. Patrimony is shown in arbitariness and favour, as in the award of scale posts; it is also typically *ritualized*. Emblems and ceremonials are used to symbolize authority relationships. This is clearly shown in the school assemblies of many secondary schools, where the most conspicuous and most active participant is the most powerful; the headteacher (King, 1973.) (However, changing authority relations are leading to changed rituals, see King, 1982). As an espouser of traditional ways such a form of assembly might have been expected of the headteacher at St George's, but no.

Mr Gordon was pleased to have 'the clergy' take school assembly. Its form showed a clear division between the sacred and the secular. After the prayers, hymns and address by the clergyman, the headteacher dealt with matters of school organization. Mr Gordon did an assembly each week, but because he didn't like staff watching him, no teacher knew directly what went on, nor was I able to observe. The teachers were pleased to have some 'free' time, but puzzled. Mr Gordon knew of their puzzlement. What did happen at his assemblies?

> All sorts of things happen. I'm certainly guilty from time to time of having the whole of my 25 minutes of assembly where nothing religious, certainly not an act of worship, nothing religious is ever mentioned. At certain times of the year there seems to be so many announcements to talk about that in fact it is just an announcements session.

Children confirmed, without my asking, that is was 'a talk' 'about anything he (Mr Gordon) likes'.

There had been a *House system* at St George's that had fallen into disuse. Mr Gordon announced the revival of the system, with a new set of names and prizes, at his assembly. The teachers heard about it incidentally from the children. Although generally in favour of the revival, some were a little put out by its management, 'not good enough really'. Staff meetings were not common; tradition assumes concensus of purpose, an assumption not always justified.

With an associated first school from which virtually all children moved on to the middle school, recruitment at Greenleigh was not a problem, although the roll had fallen in common with other schools and the national trend. (The problem of retaining pupils is dealt with in the next chapter.) The quantity of the catchment was guaranteed as was its quality. In the headteacher, Mr Kirby's, estimate 'We are very fortunate in our catchment area'. There was no remedial provision made or thought necessary. In general there were few behaviour problems (chapter 5).

Parents were supportive and cooperative (chapter 6). Soon after his appointment Mr Kirby set out to cultivate these qualities.

> Every night from the first day I was appointed I actually went out into the community for two or three hours every night, and . . . knocked on people's doors and introduced myself, and went into their homes to talk to them briefly about the fact I was the new head, and that I'd be interested in their comments about what they would like to see done, what their views were about the future, and so on, for the school and for the children.

In a new school, with 'excellent facilities', cooperative parents and able children, only the then existing teachers put limits on Mr Kirby's ambitions for change. In his recollection the core of long serving staff took the view that 'headteachers come and go but we go on for ever' in their resistance to change. Mr Kirby was at least the fourth headteacher they had had at Greenleigh, and they had recently experienced two big changes which the survey of 1971 showed they had anticipated with concern; reorganization from junior to middle school, and the move from old traditional classroomed school to the new open plan school. Mr Kirby wanted 'the quality of (children's) work . . . upped tremendously', and in recollection asked the teachers, 'these children are very capable, what can you do to make sure you are fulfilling them, if not stretching them?'

He expected them to show the qualities that might lead him to award a scale post (listed earlier in this chapter) but they had not. He tried many ways to change them, including being 'dictatorial' and through staff meetings. Dissatisfied with the weekly plan or forecast of work he asked them to submit, he centralized and standardized much of the curriculum. The Ginn Reading Scheme, the Fletcher Mathematics Programme and the Science Cards and Experiment boxes were introduced. Only specified topics were followed, and limits put on the use of television and radio. When Thomas Arnold wanted to reform Rugby School he ignored the masters and made the older boys his lieutenants (Mack, 1938.) Dissatisfied with the teachers' record keeping, Mr Kirby introduced record sheets that the children kept and which he had access to at any time. These changes did not make the teachers as he hoped 'be more educationalists and not just teachers', able to explain and justify what and why they did things, but he did know what they were doing.

With teachers who, in his view, resisted change, Mr Kirby depended on new staff for his purposes. One recent appointment was in line for the scale post, but one long serving teacher preferred not to take the early retirement he suggested. Staff turnover followed scale post holders going for promotion elsewhere. The deputy headship was vacant, the holder having gained his own headship. The scale post lower school leader became acting deputy headteacher, and pending a permanent appointment two part-time temporary appointments were made. (Parents mistakenly took me to be the new deputy). Whoever was appointed was expected to be a cooperative agent of change, by the headteacher; to be the author of a new staff handbook by the long serving teachers.

Mr Gordon, at St George', called himself the 'headmaster'; Mr Kirby at Greenleigh called himself and regarded himself as 'the headteacher'. He taught two mathematics sets and could enter any of the doorless classrooms and take over the teaching. He selected individuals and groups of children for teaching away from the rest of the class. He judged their teacher's effectiveness by comparing the quality of the work they had done for her with that they had done for him. When the teacher's performance was judged the poorer it was not because he was the headteacher but 'possibly because I am supposed to be good at the job anyway'. He had demonstrated his pedagogy by teaching half the school at a time in the hall. 'I taught all the lessons and the teachers were my assistants and did the marking and went round and checked and so on. I taught every day, all day, every subject'.

Mr Gordon did not let his staff attend his assemblies. Mr Kirby did require teachers to take assemblies, but he also led them with their attendance. Although there were prayers, readings and singing, these assemblies were lessons with the whole school, and 'it's done for the staff as well as for the children.' They could be used to standardize the curriculum content. Having talked about sayings and suggested that children start collecting them, teachers followed projects on sayings. Children were prepared for the assembly lesson. Having played a record, Mr Kirby, through question and answer established that the music was Vivaldi's *Autumn* from *The Four Seasons*, and gave some information about the composer (which was on the record sleeve). This was afterwards rehearsed by the teacher I was observing in preparation for the next assembly, where as she expected, *Autumn* was played again, and her children were amongst those who could name the piece, the composer and the colour of his hair (red).

The headteachers differed in their particular educational ideologies and in the extent to which they felt their colleagues made the ideologies real in their teaching. They had different groups of governors, but spoke of their relationships in similar terms. They found their governors generally supportive, ready to write letters to the local authority, and 'more or less content to leave curriculum matters' to the headteacher. A chairman was quoted as saying, 'You're the professionals, you know what you are doing, I think I know a bit about it, but you're the one who has the final say.' They expressed the same reservations about the political appointees among the governors. They did things more for themselves than for the school, and went in for political 'point scoring'. It could be 'a school governors' meeting with the left overs from the night before's council meeting'.

They related to the same set of local authority officials. Mr Gordon was the less satisfied in his relationship, finding them unhelpful in his problems of recruitment. They agreed about advisors. Advisors had originally been called local inspectors, and this was what they felt they had become, reporting to the chief educational officer rather than being supportive of teachers. They felt they had to conceal problems, like staff weaknesses, for fear of the consequences. Things had to be presented in an acceptable way, in a favourable light. In retrospect they had reacted to advisors' advice in . . . . 'we listened to what they had got to say, we considered it, we talked about it, rejected it, a large part of it as being . . . unworkable, so we went ahead and did our own things'.

Headteacher, Teacher, Child

We are what we do. The things that were done to be a headteacher, teacher or child at junior school, had a certain homology. Headteachers could teach anything and anybody, teachers and children. Teachers taught everything and did the most important things; mathematics, reading and writing. Children did everything. Child-centred education is teacher-centred education.

9 Junior Middle Schools: Precarious Value

The schools of this study were variants of the usual 7–11 junior schools and 8–12 middle schools. This chapter examines this kind of school at three levels; national, local, and at that of the individual schools studied. All educational innovations need the appropriate conditions for success and survival. Before these are achieved a state of what Clark (1968) called 'precarious value' exists. He applied the term to the introduction of junior colleges in California. These were open access institutions with two year courses. Part of their precarious value was their status; were they thirteenth and fourteenth grade extensions of the high school or a part of higher education? The precarious value of 8–12 middle schools also concerns their status. How do they relate to orthodox junior schools and to primary education in general?

Junior Middle Schools, Nationally

Most children in England change from primary to secondary school at the age of eleven. This pattern was advocated in the Hadow (1931) Report and made law by the 1944 Education Act. The Hadow report had advocated the separation of infants' from junior schools at seven. However, the majority of primary schools are for five to eleven year olds, with separate infants' and junior departments. What can be called *seven to eleven thinking* has been institutionalized about the nature of junior education.

The 1964 Education Act allowed the primary to secondary transition to be made at later ages than eleven, so enabling the creation of middle schools. The Plowden Report of 1967, recommended the creation of middle schools for eight to twelve year olds, with the corollary of first schools for five to eights. The main justification for first schools was as a solution to the problem of slow readers who seemed to suffer in the transition at seven. The Plowden version of the middle school is what Andy Hargreaves (1980) has called the *extension model*, an extension of the junior school.

> If the middle school is to be a new and progressive force it must develop further the curriculum, methods and attitudes which exist at present in junior schools. It must move forward into what is now regarded as secondary school work, but must not move so far away that it loses the best of primary education as we know it now.
>
> (Plowden Report, Paras. 383–4.)

Almost before any middle schools came into existence a vigorous lobby began pressing the importance and autonomy of the middle years of schooling. (For example, Schools Council Working Paper, 1969.) However, those that were created were not all of the Plowden or extension model, but for nine to thirteen-year-olds, what Hargreaves (1980) has called the 'invention model'. These were given secondary school status, although having children of traditional primary age. These schools, and others with children of eleven and younger, are discussed in chapter 10.

The reorganization of primary education into first and middle schools is in the power of local education authorities, but only with the approval of the Secretary of State for Education. About a thousand 8–12 middle schools and middle school departments (in the ratio of two to one respectively) currently exist. The number has been slowly declining in recent years as rolls have fallen, owing to a declining birth rate. The number has also fallen as some local authorities have reverted to junior schools (in Brighton and Hull) and to combined infant and junior primary schools. Seven to eleven thinking still dominates primary education; the junior middle school has precarious value.

This status is broadly conferred by a report on eight to twelve middle schools by Her Majesty's Inspectors (1985). They surveyed forty-nine schools in twenty-five local authorities. In their subjective judgment, 'Almost all the schools in the survey were pleasant places in which to live and work' (p.v.). However, only fifteen schools achieved 'satisfactory or better' standards over two thirds of the curriculum, with particular neglect of religious education, craft, design and technology, home studies and geography. HMI are not very specific in what they mean by standards or about the criteria they used to judge their level. Although they carry out social surveys, their judgments draw upon their ascribed educational wisdom. Questioning their judgments, or their basis, tends to deny the questioner's own wisdom. One of their specific recommendations, a combination of class and specialist teaching for the older children, queries the basis of the primary school tradition in middle school pedagogy; precarious value.

Junior Middle Schools of Newbridge

The Plowden Report's (1967) recommendation of 8–12 middle schools was seen at the time as a way of dealing with the logistical problems of raising the school leaving age. In Newbridge they were to solve the logistical problems of secondary reorganization. This started with a working party in 1964, which following Circular 10/65 presented the proposal of 11–16 comprehensive schools with a sixth form college. This was submitted by the education committee to the Department of Education and Science who made reservations about the small form entry to the schools and the rather academic concept of the college. Following the publication of the Plowden Report (1967) the idea of turning the infants' schools into first schools and the juniors into middle schools was seen as a way of increasing the form entry into the comprehensives by recruiting at twelve instead of eleven. The objection to the sixth form college was met by proposing the establishment of a tertiary college replacing the technical college.

The proposal was accepted by the Department of Education and Science, and in 1971 what was called 'the last 11 + in Newbridge' was held. As part of research funded by the Social Science Research Council, the headteachers and teachers of the primary schools were surveyed in the last year before reorganization, 1972, in which they were asked about their views of the change (chapter 1). In 1970, the local authority set up a middle school working party of headteachers, teachers and advisors. This met twelve times in a local community centre, and with the Director of Education's permission was attended (observed) by either my then research colleague Joan Fry or myself.

The survey and the observation of the working party showed most teachers and headteachers viewed the organization with equanimity. Most teachers anticipated teaching children of the same age as they currently did, in much the same way and in much the same conditions. There was some concern about the extra, fourth, year. Advisors urged consideration of specialist teaching, but this was resisted as being contrary to the view of the new schools using the best of primary school practice, predicated on the class teacher. In discussions of the working part the oral compromise was reached of teachers with 'specialist interest.' These already existed for music and French.

What the headteachers in particular wanted, was to claim more resources on account of their responsibility for children previously funded more favourably as secondary pupils. Two middle schools were to occupy former secondary modern schools, with laboratories and workshops. These facilities, the headteachers argued, were necessary for teachers to fulfil their specialist interest teaching in all middle schools. No funds were made available for such changes, but the local authority did decide to make capitation allowances with fourth year pupils indexed at the higher secondary level.

In 1983, ten years after the reorganization, the eighteen middle schools and middle school departments were surveyed in a partial replication of the 1972 survey (chapter 1). Only six headteachers were still in post from before reorganization, but all were asked to comment on their experience of the 8–12 system.

All the middle schools of Newbridge had a brochure or prospectus for parents, but only one made reference to anything about its being a middle school, in this seeming paraphrase of the Plowden Report.

> As a middle school we try to keep the best of the primary schools and blend it with other opportunities.

Other than send their children to independent schools, parents had no choice but middle schools; there was no point in legitimizing them. Most of the headteachers did so in the survey, mainly in the terms of the Plowden model, sometimes specifically evoked. The two linked concerns expressed before reorganization were still expressed; resources and teacher-specialization, and were related to school size. The headteachers of larger schools (300 pupils or more), thought that only such sized schools could provide sufficient specialist training. No teacher taught only one subject. Virtually all were class teachers, but in the third and particularly the fourth years, children were taught by others, particularly for French and music (as before reorganization) and mathematics. In the larger schools English, science, art and craft, and home economics were 'specialist taught'. For French, English and mathematics, these were often in sets. The headteachers of the smaller schools were more concerned about material resources; teacher specialization was limited by the lack of specialist facilities, especially for science.

With the reorganization of local government in 1974, Newbridge became part of the enlarged Nossex education authority. Seven-to-eleven thinking prevailed in Nossex, even in the areas where comprehensive secondary schools had been introduced. However, the alternative middle school for nine to thirteen-year-olds had been introduced in one area as part of secondary organization. The headteachers of Newbridge middle schools felt that the Nossex officials never really understood the eight-to-twelve system, not of their making. They were serviced by the Nossex junior school advisors, but these they felt 'never really knew what to do about the fourth year'. The education officers they thought lacked understanding, bordering on indifference and irritation with a system 'that didn't fit in', and suspected that they planned to revert to seven-to-eleven arrangements to cope with falling rolls. They suspected precarious value.

St. George's and Greenleigh — as Middle Schools

No teacher at either school was strongly in favour of junior middle schools. They had all taught in seven-to-eleven conditions; only one had been specifically trained for junior-middle school teaching. The teachers of the second and third years thought that their teaching was little different to that of the third and fourth years in seven-to-eleven organization, although 'I'll always think of them as third years' (of second years).

The loss of the first year juniors to the new first schools was not seen as a problem by the Newbridge middle school working party before reorganization, nor given particular attention by the headteachers afterwards. The first year teachers of St. George's and Greenleigh were concerned. The first years arriving from the first schools were 'second years really', but they'd been kept 'babies' by the infants' school regime. They had to work hard, and the children worked hard, to 'catch up', which they considered achieved by the end of the year, but 'some never recover'.

Before reorganization, the extra, new fourth year was much discussed, and used in the struggle for resources. At St. George's the final year had precarious value due to 'fourth-year-itis'. Teachers found the children less enthusiastic, awkward at times, and unwilling to be prefects (chapter 6). This was due to their age and 'they know they're leaving'. The longer experienced teachers recalled similar problems when children knew the results of the 11+ exam and 'they knew where they were going'.

Consistent with his espousal of traditional methods, Mr Gordon, headteacher of St. George's, expressed doubts about the eight-to-twelve arrangements, and like other heads thought the local authority could re-introduce the seven-to-eleven arrangement. Parents, he felt, did not understand the middle school system, and would prefer their children to start secondary school at eleven. A few did remove their children at the end of the third year to go to independent schools. The teachers who had done so with their own daughters said they were dissatisfied with the comprehensive schools at Newbridge and not the fourth year at St. George's.

Mr Kirby, at Greenleigh, was one of the most enthusiastic of Newbridge headteachers for the middle school arrangement. After reorganization, the Newbridge authority head set up a system of committees for each age stage of education, to deal with common problems and liaise with earlier and later stage committees. After local authority reorganization, the middle school phase committee became more a 'pressure group and self-protection group' in relation to the less enthusiastic Nossex authority. These were Mr Kirby's views. He had been elected to chair the middle school phase committee which had a core of ex-officio headteacher members. He acted as a spokesman for the committee, as high as the chief education officer.

It was a sad irony that Greenleigh, whose headteacher was among the most enthusiastic of middle school proponents, should be the most precarious of Newbridge middle schools. Before secondary reorganization, Greenleigh children not awarded grammar school places in Newbridge would sometime apply and gain places at a nearby school under the control of the Nossex authority. The headteacher of Oldbury school was interviewed in 1968 as part of a survey of secondary schools (King, 1973). He expressed satisfaction in taking these out-county Greenleigh children. Oldbury became an eleven to eighteen comprehensive school and, after local authority reorganization, in the same new Nossex authority as Greenleigh. Greenleigh children continued to transfer to Oldbury rather than Newbridge comprehensives, but at the age of twelve rather than the usual age of eleven. A further survey of secondary schools in 1978 (King, 1982) showed the new headteacher of Oldbury valued these Greenleigh children, creating a separate second year class for them.

The 1980 Education Act extended parents' choice of their children's school. The recently appointed headteacher of Oldbury let parents know through ex-Greenleigh children that the changed law allowed them to choose to send any other children to his school at eleven. The news soon spread, and in consequence the size of the Greenleigh fourth year was halved. Mr Kirby, the governors and the local authority were powerless to do anything about it. Mr Kirby did not see the parents' action as a rejection of the middle school scheme or the new fourth year in particular, but a rejection of the comprehensive system of Newbridge, with short course schools and tertiary college. Their preference, he thought, was for an integral sixth form, and only incidently for transfer at eleven. Some first year children at Greenleigh anticipated leaving for Oldbury at the end of the third year. The fourth year children were given some extra privileges and started the year at a residential fields studies centre to help generate group sentiment.

Seven-to-eleven thinking among teachers, local authorities, parents and children resists change and ascribes precarious value to middle schools. Their place in the total system of primary education is considered in the next and final chapter.

10   The Nature and Diversity of Primary Education

The research of this book is over and its reporting done. This final chapter puts it into some of the contexts outlined in the first chapter, to consider the nature of primary education largely from a sociological perspective. To write of 'primary education' implies a spurious unity in increasing diversity. 'Primary schools' may be for children aged 5–7, 5–8, 5–9, 5–10, 5–11, 5–12, 7–11 and 8–12, whilst children of primary school age may attend secondary schools for 9–13 or 10–13-year-olds. These different age ranges are one of the elements of the diversity of primary education. An attempt will be made to sketch the dimensions of this variability in terms of the social characteristics of teachers and children, which are for the most part independent of them as individuals. This will draw upon the available data, mainly from research, not all sociological.

The style of research of this book, single-handed, mainly qualitative and close up to those studied, means that its reporting becomes rather autobiographical; an account of what the author did during a sketch of his or her professional life. The final section is an epilogue on this theme.

Sociological Perspectives on Primary Education

The 'new' sociologists of education of the early seventies (for example Gorbutt, 1972) described the theories of what they called the 'orthodox' sociology of education as being based on structural functionalism. As Bernstein (1973) has pointed out, this was not entirely true, although structural functionalism was the dominant theoretical perspective in sociology throughout the fifties and early sixties, under the influence of the American Talcott Parsons (1902–1979). We are fortunate to have an analysis of primary education by this eminent theorist. The new sociology of education soon factionalized, and one faction, the neo-Marxist, has produced an analysis of primary education (Sharp and Green, 1975). Both analyses are of specific areas of primary education, but their explanations are more generally applicable. They will be examined through the neo-Weberian perspective of this research.

Parsons's (1961) essay, 'The school class as social system: some of its functions in American society', makes particular reference to the elementary school class, the US equivalent of a British primary school class. A footnote says that its principle source was a study carried out with Samuel A. Stouffer and Florence R. Kluckhohn, 'Unfortunately the material is not available in published form'. Confusingly, the research was 'among boys (*sic*) in the public high schools (*sic*) in the Boston metropolitan area'.

Parsons defined a social system as a 'plurality of individual actors interacting with one another, (Parsons *et al*, 1953). This sounds like an acceptable definition of social structure as used throughout this study, but Parsons's system is more than this; it is the association of the structure of social relationships with the functions or outcomes of those relationships — hence structural-functionalism. Every social system must solve four basic 'problems' for its adequate maintenance. These are adaptation and goal-attainment in relation to external systems, integration and latency, the maintenance of internal patterns of shared values. These problems exist for all systems from the social system (society) figuratively downwards, so that all structured forms and their functions are basically alike. From this it follows that there is a fundamental similarity between an education system, the individual schools, the classrooms, and even the individual teacher-pupil dyad, the smallest social system.

These abstract systems problems are alluded to in the essay on the elementary school classroom, 'From the point of view of society [the school class is] an agency of manpower'. This is the school class adapting to the needs of society. Education 'functions to internalize in its pupils both the commitments and capacities of their future adult roles and . . . functions to allocate these human resources within the role-structure of society'. This perhaps is latency in school leading to goal-attainment outside school.

This is not the place to make an extended critique of Parsonian structural-functionalism, particularly after so brief a presentation. However, a number of points should be made about its adequacy as a theory of primary education. First there is the tendency towards reification, where social structures, the relationships between people, are regarded as non — or extra — human things. Systems, including schools and classrooms, can't have problems or seek to fulfil goals, only people may define situations as problems or have goals. The 'pattern maintenance' and related 'tension management' of pupils, that is their social control, maybe a problem for their teachers but not necessarily for the children (chapter 5). This points to the implicit consensus that is part of Parson's analysis; conflict is absent or minimal because of the assumption of patterns of shared values among teachers and children. In Parson's analysis the meanings of the actions of children (and teachers) are of little account as they are socialized, selected and allocated to meet the needs of the higher-order occupational system according to their largely psychological properties of intelligence and achievement motivation. They are in Garfinkel's (1967) phrase 'cultural dopes', filled up with consensual values which lead them to regard the system as 'fair'.

Despite its limitations structural-functionalism does make at least one important point about schools, they are not 'closed' systems, but 'open' ones. If we put people back into the physical imagery of systems, we can say that the relationships between teachers and children which constitute the social structure of 'the school' are not the only ones they have, expect to have or know about. Primary age children do not (legally) follow paid employment, but they relate to those who do, teachers, parents and others, and have a consciousness of the occupational structure or system. The 'adaptation' of primary education to this 'external system' is not made directly by employers coming into the schools, but through kin relationships and extra-school acquired consciousness (chapter 2). There is discensus, if not conflict, about primary schooling as an 'agency of manpower' (*sic*); this is the children's view but not their teachers.

The empirical basis of Parson's essay is not very clear, but that of Rachel Sharp and Tony Green's study (with Jacqueline Lewis) (1975) is clearer. They studied three (of four) teachers in the infants' department of a 5–11 school, and the headteacher. Their main method was the use of 'probing' interviews, and although observations (by three observers using three different methods) were used, they report few descriptions of classroom events. The authors started out using a phenomenological perspective, but their study has all the elements of neo-Marxist theory, which David Hargreaves (1978) has suggested did not arise from the research but were applied retrospectively.

In the absence of the once-predicted revolution, neo-Marxists pose a basically functionalist explanation of structures in capitalist societies, as perpetuating those societies. Hence, Sharp and Green's conclusion that progressive infants' education is conservative in perpetuating the existing capitalist order. The continued existence of capitalism is also explained by false consciousness — that workers do not know their 'true' interests, the overthrow of capitalism. Thus Sharp and Green largely ignore the explanations the teachers gave of their practices. The material determinism of their Marxism is shown in their proposal that the teachers' pedagogy was not an expression of their ideology (false consciousness) but of the material conditions of overcrowded classes. There is a further convergence with Parsons's (1951) structural functional analysis of education (which Sharp and Green criticize), in their regarding teachers' assessments of children's work as an early stage in the process of selection and allocation to the occupational structure.

In my research (King, 1978), a few teachers were defined by their headteachers as not being 'proper infants' teachers'. They did do things differently to their colleagues. They were aware of their being different, and they and their headteachers attributed this to their not being 'infant trained'. This contradicts Sharp and Green's view that material constraints, rather than ideology, accounts for infants' teachers' pedagogy. These teachers worked in the same material conditions as their colleagues, but taught differently because of their non-acceptance of elements of the professional ideology of their colleagues. The teachers in the present study who showed low commitment worked in the same conditions as their colleagues; their dissent was ideological (chapter 7). Sharp and Green's analysis of Mapledene School traduces infants' education. Their conclusions could be applied to any form of education (including those of non-capitalist societies). They explain nothing that is special about primary education, infants' education or the particular school they studied.

Structural-functionalism and Marxism fail to provide an adequate analysis of primary education. They are what Weber (1948) regarded as emanationist theories, where the nature of society is known *a priori* to any investigation. Primary education is explained hypostatically by the determining higher order system or capitalist economy that it rests upon. The subjectivities of teachers and children who relate together to create primary education are of little account. They are either cultural dopes or suffering false consciousness.

Primary education is a large scale or *macro-structure*; the pattern of relationships between some 155,000 teachers and 3½ million children in nearly 20,000 schools. (Statistics of Education, 1985). Collins (1981) takes the view that macro-structures consist of aggregates of *micro-structures*. The micro-structures of primary education, are groups of a teacher and children in classrooms and schools. We can never encounter primary education except in the micro-situation of school and classroom. Macro-sociological concepts, like primary education, can only be made fully empirical by grounding them in a sample of typical micro-events that make them up. Parsons and Sharp and Green did encounter the micro-structures of primary education but ignored them in theorizing about the macro-structure. According to Weber (1958) any causal explanations of social behaviour should be *'adequate at the level of meaning'*. This is part of the process of *Verstehen*. Only in micro-situations, in classrooms of schools, can a sociologist enter his subjects' social world of commonsense constructs and experience (Leat, 1972).

To speak of primary education is to make generalizations about the typical relationships between a large number of teachers and children. Most of these generalizations should also apply in the various micro-situations of school and classroom. All situations consist of three elements; structural (the patterns of relationships between people as they relate to one another), material (the condition of the place where they relate), and subjective (their interests, ideas and beliefs in so relating) (King, 1985). The distinctive social elements of primary education consist of a structure of stable groups of young children of similar age, learning the same things, taught by one teacher most of the time, in a particular space (classroom), over a period of a year. The teacher's pedagogy is based on definitions of the nature of children and their learning capacities; they learn for their own benefit in the here and now, an intrinisic evaluation that the children may not share.

Primary education is fundamentally holistic. Children's learning is an unspecialized whole, they are taught by one teacher the whole time. Primary education is a common cultural experience. Children learn and so share the same things; they share the experience of learning the same things. For adults, their primary education is one experience they hold in common with most others. Primary education, uncoupled from direct contact with the occupational structure, is the most important institution of common cultural transmission.

Primary education is not independent of other social structures. That children from middle class homes tend to be more successful in their learning than those from working class homes, may suggest that it is a middle class institution, but this would be true of virtually all elements of the educational system, not only in Britain but in other capitalist societies, and non-capitalist ones too (King, 1987). The special nature of primary education is predicated upon the ideologies of those who daily control relationships to create its structure — the teachers.

The common element in primary teachers' professional ideologies is *child-centredness*; in the words of the Plowden Committee (1967), 'At the heart of the education process lies the child'. Children are seen as passing through a naturally ordered sequence of physical, physiological, psychological and social development, whilst each child processes a unique individuality. Education is seen as creating the conditions which acknowledge these qualities and allow the full development of individual potential.

However, to anticipate the following discussion on the diversity of primary education, it is again proposed (as in chapter 2) that there are two principal professional ideologies of primary education. They are not rivals, they are sequential — those of infants' and juniors' education. In my research, both infants' and junior teachers expressed what is special and different about themselves and other groups. The two kinds of teachers are educated separately and differently. Their practices have separate and different origins and histories. Developmentalism and individualism are common ideological elements of the two groups, but play-as-learning and childhood innocence are special to infants' education. Among junior school teachers developmentalism operates with a psychometric paradigm. Children's rates of cognitive development are made finite; some will never be as 'able' as others. As I have tried to show, the ideologies not only define the nature of children and their learning, but the nature of being their teacher.

The Diversity of Primary Education

A major theme of this chapter, and indeed this book, is that there are (at least) two primary educations; infants' and juniors. Seven-to-eleven thinking (chapter 9) is part of five-to-seven-to-eleven thinking, institutionalized since the 1944 Education Act. For twenty years after the Act these ages were the sole time markers in the structure of primary education, and continue to be so throughout most of the country. However, now children may be changing school at any age from seven to thirteen, with some children of conventionally primary school age attending secondary schools.

A corollary of introducing middle schools has been first schools. The 'Plowden Model' is for five to eight-year-olds. Like the associated eight to twelve middle schools it is an extension model, an extended infants' school. This was the view of the Plowden Committee in their recommendation, and that of infants' headteachers at Newbridge faced with the prospect of the change (King, 1978). Middle Schools for 9–13 are associated with first schools for 5–9's.

The introduction of first schools has not created the same interest as that of middle schools, and fewer studies have been made of them. How do the three kinds of school for young children differ, other than by age-range? Her Majesty's Inspectors (1982) take the view that, 'There are marginal differences between these two kinds of (first) school and others with the more traditional age ranges'. This may be so in terms of the limited and often unexplicated criteria used by HMI in their evaluations, but their own limited survey results do show differences that may be significant. The 'main phase experience' of teachers in 5–8 schools was mainly (63 per cent) in infants' schools, only 10 per cent in junior schools, compared with 46 and 25 per cent, respectively, in 5–9 schools. This may have followed from the origins of the schools, most 5–8 schools were formerly infants' schools (73 per cent — all of those in Newbridge), but most 5–9 were formerly junior with infants' (5–11) schools (68 per cent). This may also explain why 46 per cent of the headteachers of 5–8 schools were formerly infants' heads and 30 per cent formerly combined school heads (one of eighteen in Newbridge), compared with 13 and 40 per cent, respectively, for 5–9 schools.

The Newbridge planning committee thought that it would be a 'good thing' if more men were on the staff of the new 5–8 schools, usually with reference to playing football (King, 1978). The Department of Education and Science statistics show this to have been fulfilled nationally. Men form 1.5 per cent of infants' school teachers, but 12.2 per cent in first schools. The statistics do not distinguish between 5–8 and 5–9 schools, but we might expect the proportion to be higher in the latter. The headships of infants' schools are very much the preserve of women, with men holding only 2.3 per cent of posts (but still a larger proportion than women). However, 33.5 per cent of first school headships are held by men. Just as the declining number of girls' secondary schools brought about by comprehensive reorganization is associated with reduced chances of headships for women, so also has the reorganization of infants' to first schools.

Do these differences in staff sex and experience indicate differences in educational practices? I have already referred to those Newbridge teachers whose headteachers defined as not being 'proper infants' teachers' having been junior trained. Have junior school practices been introduced into first schools where a substantial minority of staff have junior experience, and more importantly where the headteacher has a junior school background? Structural indices might be the introduction of setting, most probably for mathematics, for older children with subject timetabling. Pedagogically, there might be greater use of direct control signalling the end of innocence. These changes are more likely to have happened in the 5–9 schools.

It could be that first schools, especially the 5–9 kind, are sites of ideological tension between infants' and junior school factions. Not that this is necessarily new. Similar tension may exist between the infants' and junior departments of 5–11, and between the first and middle departments of 5–12 and 5–13 schools, where since the headteachers are predominately men (5–11, 74.1 per cent, 5–12, 84.1 and 5–13, 88.3) they are also likely to be junior trained. It would be wrong to infer that these possible tensions are gender-based; they would be related to differences in initial education. The few men infants' teachers I observed, worked in ways similar to their women colleagues, the only conspicuous difference was their restraint in physical contact with the children, for what one called 'obvious reasons' (King, 1978).

There may be few if any significant differences in the pedagogies of men and women infants'-first school teachers, but the nature of the education they provide is probably related to the large proportion of women teachers. The ideologue-founders of infants' education were predominately women (Whitbread, 1972). In my research experience, infants-first schools are less bureaucratized, through meetings and paper, than junior-middle schools, and the staff show a higher degree of colleagiality. Research outside primary education suggests an association between teachers' socio-sexual identities (gender) and their disposition towards bureaucratic organization. Gross and Trask (1976) found men principals of American elementary schools reported more satisfaction with their administrative tasks than did women. Easthope (1975) found that women in English secondary schools reported more feelings of estrangement in the bureacracy of larger schools than did men. My survey of secondary schools showed that it was in those with predominantly male staffs that administration was most important, in terms of posts, scale points and meetings (King, 1982). Girls' schools had the highest proportion of women with positions of responsibility, but were less bureaucratized. You don't have to be a feminist to see this as another aspect of *patriarchy* (male dominance). Infants' schools may be bastions of what could be called *matriarchy*.

Nursery schools and *nursery classes* (attached to infants' or combined schools) are not new, and may be regarded as part of the infants' education tradition (Whitbread, 1972). The little expansion that occurred has often been a part of 'compensatory education' programmes, as shown in Hartley's (1985) Scottish study. A post-war innovation has been the growth of confusingly called *'pre-school education'*. Nursery and pre-school education (the many forms are reviewed by Northam, 1983) have introduced many children to elements of the materials and methods of infants' reception classes, particularly play-as-learning. Pre-school playgroups were originally the initiative of middle-class mothers but they are being spread to working class areas too, so that more children may be finding the reception class activities all too familiar. Some infants' teachers regard an adequate experience of classroom play as a pre-requisite for further learning (King, 1978). It could be that this earlier experience of adult organized play may lead to the earlier introduction of more formal learning in school.

The teaching methods of infants' teachers have attracted less research interest that those of juniors. Bennett and his associates' (1976) typology of junior teachers was produced by a cluster-analysis of teachers' self-reported practices. The ideal typical most 'progressive' teacher favoured integration of subject matter, allowed children choice of work, whether in groups or individually, choice of seating, some freedom of movement and talk, used little assessment by testing, and favoured 'intrinsic motivation' — in my research experience, a typical infants' teacher. 'Informal' approaches may be typical of infants' teachers but not universal, as a controversy over a Surrey headteacher showed (reported in *The Observer,* 31 August 1986, 'Heads roll in parent revolt'). Her introduction of such standard infants' practices as sand and water play, lego construction and dressing up, led to some parents protesting.

Informal methods might be thought to correspond to Bernstein's (1975) 'invisible pedagogy', 'a particular form of pre-school/infant school pedagogy'. Unfortunately, we are not told what other forms there are. Karabel and Halsey (1977) are wrong in referring to this paper as being based on research. A secondary analysis of my own empirical data lead to the conclusion that the invisible pedagogy could not be found (King, 1979). According to Berstein the pedagogy is predicated upon a particular 'knowledge code'. This theory of codes is a self-sustained academic conceit, which may in time be regarded as being as quaint as MacDougall's (1908) hormic theory of human behviour. Both theories purport to explain much but explain nothing, there being little or no empirical evidence for the real existence of either instincts or codes.

Much of the research of junior age education has been searches for best methods. Bennett and his associates (1976) concluded that children taught formally tended to make more progress than those taught informally. The interest this conclusion created was partly due, as the Radical Statistics Groups (1982) point out, to extensive pre-publication publicity. In the analysis the progress was of 335 children taught by 13 teachers classified as formal, 295 taught by 12 classified as mixed, and 321 taught by 12 informal teachers. None of these aggregates of data represents a real teaching/learning group. The 335 children were never collectively taught by the 13 formal teachers (King, 1980). The data were socially decontextualized. The analysis obscured the possibility that teachers similarly classified could produce different levels of progress, so that the broad conclusion must be doubted. This kind of research is heavily dependent of the method of analysis. The data has been reanalyzed and different conclusions reached (Aitken, Bennett and Hesketh, 1981). Bennett (1987) has recently stated, 'The theory underpinning the *Teaching Styles* study is dead'.

Bennett *et al*'s typology of teaching methods was based upon a cluster analysis of teachers' self-reported practices. Galton, Simon and Cross (1980) criticize this. Their own cluster analysis was of observed teacher behaviour, as part of Observational Research and Classroom Learning Evaluation (ORACLE). Each was observed 45 times for 25 seconds, a total of 19 minutes. Each of the titles of the books reporting ORACLE includes the phrase 'in the primary classroom'. Such snippets of observation were gathered in the classrooms of 8 to 10-year-olds in junior schools, 8–12 middle schools and 9–13 middle schools (not primary schools).

As with Bennett *et al* (1976), the data were socially decontextualized in the analysis. Cluster analyses produced a four-fold typology of pupils and a six-fold one of teachers, based upon observations of the behaviour of eight children in each of 58 teachers' classes. However, all the data reported are for false aggregates of children taught by all the teachers of a particular type, so that, for example, the nine 'class enquirer' teachers never taught their 76 pupils together. It is therefore possible that all seven 'intermittent worker' children could have been taught by the same teacher, representing 87.5 per cent (seven of eight) of a real group sample, rather than the 9.2 per cent of the false aggregate. But this type of pupil is supposed to be most commonly associated with the individual monitor type teacher, representing 47.6 per cent of the false aggregate. It should be stressed that an aggregate is only false (or 'true') in relation to the explanation posed. Basically, we must not lose sight of the real people in their relationships in real groups and situations when performing calculations on data about them. They should be visible in every table of results. Like that of Delphi, the ORACLE may be obscurely misleading.

Jencks and his associates' (1973) statistical analysis of American data led them to conclude that variations in educational attainment were largely unrelated to variations in educational provisional, mainly in economic and material terms. This much publicized conclusion was vulgarized into 'Schools don't count'. Rutter, Maughan, Mortimore and Ouston (1979) using a sample of twelve secondary schools claimed to have refuted this. The Inner London Education Authority Junior School Project follows similar methods, the senior author being Peter Mortimore (1987). The substantial sample is of approximately 2000 children in fifty schools, studied over four years. If Bennett *et al* (1976) and Galton *et al* (1980) were engaged in the hunt for the 'good' teacher, Mortimore's hunt is for the 'good' school.

The use of schools as basic units of analysis maintains real groups. The Bennett *et al* (1976) and Galton *et al* (1980) studies reveal little about the social location of different kinds of teaching. My research suggests that teachers' methods are similar within schools. This was so for the three-infants-first schools (King, 1978) and for Greenleigh and St. George's. The differences were between schools not within. This is not surprising Teachers in a given school teach children with similar characteristics, in similar material conditions under the authority of the same headteacher.

Unfortunately, although Mortimore *et al* (1987) reach conclusions about the differences between schools, their analyses are not always based on appropriately aggregated data — they do not always deal with real groups. Teachers were asked to assess the children they taught for being above or below average ability. But the analysis is of an aggregate of the assessments of all the teachers. Most of the children and teachers were unknown to one another, and who was assessing who is unknowable. The authors conclude, 'it is clear that schools do make a difference and that difference is substantial'. The conclusion may be correct, but not clearly so.

How do the different kinds of school for older primary age children differ, other than by age range; 5–11, 5–12, 7–11, 8–12, 9–13 and 10–13? The national and local (to Newbridge) origins and characteristics of 8–12, junior–middle, Plowden extension model schools were discussed in chapter 9. The 9–13 middle schools have attracted more attention. Hargreaves (1980) calls this the invention model. Nationally there are roughly equal numbers of middle schools designated secondary (mainly 9–13, some 10–13), and middle schools, designated primary (8–12), although being bigger, more children attend the former, and unlike the latter the number of schools and pupils is slightly increasing. The protagonists of the 9–13 school face what Lynch (1980) regards as a 'legitimation crisis'. How, having been created for administrative convenience to cope with material and economic extingencies (limited money, existing buildings, changing child population, secondary reorganization), may they be educationally justified, other than being a 'transit camp' hybrid, with both primary and secondary characteristics? Another case of precarious value? (chapter 9).

The studies of teaching styles and schools effectiveness are of limited help in comparisons of the two kinds of middle school and junior schools. Better, are less statistically sophisticated surveys by Barker Lunn (1982), and by Taylor and Garson (1982). The professional experience of teachers in the two types of middle school are markedly different. In Taylor and Garson's (1982) survey most (66.9 per cent) of teachers' in 8–12 schools previous experience had been confined to primary schools; few had only secondary experience (3.5 per cent). Similar proportions existed in Newbridge (68 and 4 per cent respectively), where apart from redeployment cases, the local authority policy was not to appoint those with only secondary experience. In the 9–13 schools the ratio of primary experience only to secondary was 26.2 to 36.1 per cent. These schools had other secondary characteristics, with more designated specialist teachers, more often teaching only 'their' subject, that is, less single class teaching. Ability setting for subjects was more common, as was regular homework. These structures have real consequences for children's educational experience. For example, a ten-year-old in a 9–13 school is twice as likely to be taught by mathematics specialist than one in an 8–12 school, and a nine-year-old in a 9–13 school is twice as likely to be taught French than one in an 8–12 school.

Andy Hargreaves (1986) studied two middle schools, one for 9–13-year-olds, the other 10–13. He writes of their having 'two cultures of schooling'. These cultures are not a whole way of life, but the teachers' professional cultures, shared work experiences and practices. Teachers constitute a status group with class characteristics, in Weber's (1948) use of the terms in that they occupy a particular position in the economic order in terms of remuneration and conditions of work. This class embedded status group has sub groups. Among primary school teachers I have suggested the division is between infants' and junior (including junior-middle) school teachers. In 9–13 middle schools the status of groups of Hargreaves's two cultures are those of junior school and secondary school teaching. The difference (as Hargreaves suggests) is one of professional ideology, which between teachers in school leads to ideologically based tension if not conflict. The child-centred, ability differentiated junior school model prevails for the younger children, the subject-centred ability differentiated secondary school model for older children; the persistence of seven-to-eleven thinking (chapter 9).

Unfortunately, it is not clear how the two types of middle school correspond to junior schools, but, as may be expected, the evidence indicates stronger resemblances to the 8–12 type. Both have similar proportions of women teachers (junior 65.5 and 8–12, 64.4 per cent, compared with 53.9 in 9–13 schools) and women headteachers (15.9, 15.9 and 11.7 per cent respectively). Barker Lunn does not distinguish between the two types of middle school in her survey, but concludes that their organization is similar to junior schools of the same size. As junior middle schools cover a similar size range as orthodox junior schools it might be concluded they have more organizational resemblances than the typically larger 9–13 schools.

Do teaching styles vary with the age-range of the school? Galton *et al*'s (1980) sample was drawn from junior, 8–12 and 9–13 of the middle schools, but they report no differences in teaching by age-range of school. No analysis was made, or at least presented, presumably because, as the titles of their books suggest, it was assumed there were no differences to be found — they were all examples of 'The (*sic*) Primary Classroom'. This may also explain why there seems to have been no analysis of teaching styles by the professional experience of teachers. Hargreaves's (1986) study would suggest differences in the 9–13 schools between the junior and secondary teacher factions.

Bennett *et al* (1976) investigated teachers' style and pupils' progress in English and mathematics. It is not clear in which lessons Galton *et al* made their observations. Mine showed marked differences in teaching style by subject. Physical education and mathematics lessons are not taught in the same way, except at a high level of generality — under the control of the teacher. Both Bennett *et al* and Galton *et al*, seem to treat teaching style almost as an individual teacher personality characteristic, that manifests itself in any social, material or subject conditions (socially decontextualized). The studies by Delamont (1976) and Ted Wragg (1972) showed secondary teachers style to vary by their teaching subjects. Individual primary teachers probably have a range of styles, according to the subject taught. Child-centred learning follows subject-centred teaching.

Primary schools are comprehensive schools, and despite the 1980 Education Act's giving parents more choice of school, usually neighbourhood schools, (St. George's was rather exceptional, chapter 6), and so vary in their social composition of the pupil members. Does this have consequences for their school experience, in terms of process and practice? Teachers do make imputations about the children's home background, and use their definitions in typifying and explaining individual children and 'children in this school' (chapter 7). The differences between Greenleigh and St. George's were related to the teachers' group typifications of 'children in this school'. But as the research has shown, material conditions and the headteachers' particular educational ideologies were also important.

Ther NFER survey for the Plowden Report (1967) found few examples of non-streaming in schools serving middle class areas, suggesting that the innovation was then being introduced in an attempt to solve what was being defined as pupil underachievement and/or poor behaviour. These motives were often behind the introduction of mixed ability groups into secondary schools (King, 1983). Given the current widespread use of mixed ability groups in junior and junior-middle schools reported by Barker Lunn (1982), this association with social composition may not hold any more, but what of the social distribution of the 'ability' classes she refers to? Are remedial classes more common in working class areas, and enrichment classes more common in middle class areas? No child in the remedial classes of mainly working class St. George's could be classified middle class by fathers' occupation. Enrichment classes had been run at mainly middle class Greenleigh for 'gifted' children. These had been abandoned because of ill-feeling among the children, and the unacceptable lobbying of parents for their children to be selected for the class.

Do classroom practices vary with pupil social composition? The Bennett (1976) study showed that the children in his sample taught by teachers defined as informal, had lower average measured ability than those taught by other style teachers. Given the statistical association between social class and measured intelligence, this suggests that they were more often working rather than middle class in origin. Are 'progressive' methods introduced as a solution to a defined problem of underachievement? Not if Greenleigh and St. George's are any indication. By Bennett's typology the teaching style at the former was fairly informal (a term never used by the teachers). At the latter, where some (mainly working class) children were defined as underachieving, the predominant style was described as 'traditional', and corresponded to Bennett's more formal type.

Galton and Simon (1980) claim that 'socio-economic' status (of pupils) . . . did not seem (*sic*) to vary in any systematic fashion between teaching styles'. However, an inspection of their reported results show that the group instructor style was used almost twice as often as the individual monitor style with children of semi- and unskilled manual workers, whilst the individual monitor style was used three times more often than the infrequent changes style with children of professional and managerial workers. Galton and Simon are reluctant to relate their styles to any dimension of formality/informality, but there is at least a hint of what others think of as informality is a more common experience of middle class children.

Are there curriculum differences related to the social class composition of schools? In Ashton *et al*'s (1975) survey, primary school teachers in schools with mainly middle class catchments, stressed 'intellectual' development as an aim: those of working class catchments, 'social' development. How may these different aims be fulfilled? Anyon's (1981) study of American ten-year-olds in different schools concluded, 'School knowledge in the fifth grade in this affluent professional school was more abundant, difficult, analytical, and conceptual than the knowledge in the working class school'. This sounds more like mainly middle class Greenleigh than mainly working class St. George's.

Bernstein (1975) regards his elusive invisible pedagogy as being particularly advantageous to the children of what he admits is an ill-defined 'new middle class'. Whatever the social distribution of pedagogies, Bernstein (1961) in his earlier work thought informal methods inappropriate for lower working class children, who would benefit more from formal methods. 'The passivity of the working class pupil makes him (*sic*) particularly receptive of drill methods, but resistant to active participation and cooperation . . .' Their teachers do rate them less favourably for behaviour and work (especially the boys) than middle class children, and rate them slower settling in (again, especially boys) (chapter 5). We do not have the information to know if they are more favourably assessed when treated more formally. In America, compensatory education programmes for younger children have typically used 'drill' techniques (for example, Bereiter and Engelmann, 1966), some using Bernstein's early work as their justification.

Compensatory education in this country and in the United States is often that of ethnic minority children, (minorities nationally — sometimes the majority in a school). The ILEA project (Mortimore *et al*, 1987) documented their progress but indicated few differences in their teaching. Hartley's (1985) study of a Scottish primary school with a substantial proportion of children of Asian origin, shows how teachers' definitions of children's ethnicity had educational consequences.

It is commonplace to point to the diversity of secondary comprehensive schools, and to debate and investigate their supposed advantages and disadvantages. But it is this secondary diversity that is an important cause of the structural diversity sketched here. More research is required if the sketch is to be turned into a picture.

'What's to Come is Still Unsure'

It would be foolhardy to make predictions about the future of primary education, but even in uncertainty we can have cautious expectations.

Child-centred, class teacher practice is under some pressure, eroded by financially advantageous specialist teaching. The implementation of the 1988 Education Reform Act is likely to further destructure relationships. The specification of curriculum requirements could be used to justify specialist teaching. The versatility of class teachers is already strained by music and science; now they face teaching technology. Seven-to-eleven thinking is part of the introduction of national achievement tests; middle and first schools are likely to be more precarious.

A centralized, standardized curriculum and assessment system is likely to increase the use of formal methods. Bringing children to the test at seven may reduce the use of learning through play; importance will be given to that which is assessed. The intrinsic valuation of education for children in the here and now, is politically weak. Primary education for their future occupations and the State's economic condition is a reversion to the spirit of elementary education, which almost evaporated in 1944. Future HMI reports may find primary schools more efficient, productive and effective, but may be less likely to find them 'pleasant places in which to live and work'.

Is there any comfort in thinking that no-one would have made this kind of speculation ten years ago? 'What's to come is still unsure'.

When I started to write this book I knew that my state of health made it likely that I would be unable to do again the kind of research reported here; I now know that is so. In the context of my professional life, this is my last work. In the context of a changing primary education, I hope it may make a contribution to the understanding of current practice, for practitioners and sociologists alike. A colleague in another institution sent me some of his teaching material dealing with my infants' schools research (1978) which he referred to as 'sociology with a human face'. Primary education *is* the relationships between teachers and children; its humanity should be there in the research, in its doing and purpose.

Bibliography

AITKIN, M., BENNETT, S.N. and HESKETH, J. (1981) 'Teaching styles and pupil progress: A re-analysis', *British Journal of Educational Psychology*, **51**.

ANYON, J. (1981) 'Social class and school knowledge', *Curriculum Enquiry*, **11**, 1.

ASHTON, P.M.E. *et al* (1975) *The Aims of Primary Education*, Macmillan.

BARKER LUNN, J. (1970) *Streaming in Primary Schools*, NFER.

BARKER LUNN, J. (1982) 'Junior Schools and their organisational policies', *Educational Research*, **24**, 4.

BARKER LUNN, J. (1984) 'Junior school teachers: their methods and practices', *Educational Research*, **26**, 3.

BASSEY, M. (1978) *Nine Hundred Primary School Teachers*, NFER.

BELL, C. (1969) 'A note on participant observation', *Sociology*, **3**, 3.

BENNETT, S.N. (1987) 'After "Teaching Styles and Pupil Progress": Issues in dissemination and theory development', in WALFORD, G. (Ed.), *Doing Sociology of Education*, Falmer Press.

BENNETT, S.N. *et al* (1976) *Teaching Styles and Pupil Progress*, Open Books.

BENNETT, S.N., ANDREAE, J., HEGARTY, P. and WADE, B. (1980) *Open Plan Schools*, NFER.

BEREITER, C. and ENGELMANN, S. (1966) *Teaching Disadvantaged Children in Pre-School*, Prentice Hall.

BERNSTEIN, B.B. (1961) 'Social class and linguistic development: A theory of social learning', in HALSEY, A.H. *et al* (Eds), *Education, Economy and Society*, Free Press.

BERNSTEIN, B.B. (1973) *Class Codes and Control, Vol. 1*, Routledge and Kegan Paul.

BERNSTEIN, B.B. (1975) 'Class pedagogies: visible and invisible'; 'The sociology of education: A brief account', in *Class Codes and Control, Vol. 3*, Routledge and Kegan Paul.

BEYNON, J. (1987) *Initial Encounters in the Secondary School*, Falmer Press.

BLAKEMORE, K. and COOKSEY, B. (1981) *A Sociology of Education for Africa*, Allen and Unwin.

BLYTH, W.A.L. (1960) 'The sociometric study of children's groups in English schools', *British Journal of Educational Studies*.

BRANDIS, W. and BERNSTEIN, B.B. (1974) *Selection and Control*, Routledge and Kegan Paul.

BRONFENBRENNER, U. (1958) 'Socialization and social class through time and space', in MACCOBY, E.E. *et al* (Eds), *Readings in Social Psychology*, Methuen, 1958.

BURSTALL, C., JAMIESON, M., COHEN, S. and HARGREAVES, M. (1974) *Primary French in the Balance*, NFER.

CENTRAL ADVISORY COUNCIL, (1967) *Children and Their Primary Schools* (Plowden Report), HMSO.

CLARK, B.R. (1968) 'Institutionalization of innovation in higher education', *Administrative Science Quarterly*, **47**.

CLARRINCOATES, K. (1980) 'The importance of being Ernest, Emma, Jane. . .', in DEEM, R. (Ed.), *Schooling for Women's Work*, Routledge and Kegan Paul.

COLLINS, R. (1975) *Conflict Sociology*, Academic Press.

COLLINS, R. (1981) 'The micro-foundations of macro-sociology', *American Journal of Sociology*, **86**.

CULLINGFORD, C. (1985) 'The idea of the school', in *Parents, Teachers and Schools*, Royce.

CULLINGFORD, C. (1986) 'I suppose learning your tables could help you get a job', *Education 3–13*, **14**, 2.

DAVIE, R., BUTLER, N. and GOLDSTEIN, H. (1972) *From Birth to Seven*, NCDS.

DAVIES, B. (1982) *Life in the Classroom and Playground*, Routledge and Kegan Paul.

DAVIS, A. (1943) *Social Class Influence Upon Learning*, Harvard University Press.

DELAMONT, S. (1976) 'Beyond Flanders' fields', in STUBBS, M. and DELAMONT, S. (Eds), *Explorations in Classroom Observation*, Wiley.

DELMAINE, J. (1979) 'IQism as ideology and the political economy of education', *Educational Studies*, **5**.

DEPARTMENT OF EDUCATION AND SCIENCE (1982) Education 5–9, HMSO.

DEPARTMENT OF EDUCATION AND SCIENCE (1985) Statistics of Education, HMSO.

DEPARTMENT OF EDUCATION AND SCIENCE (1985) Education 8–12, HMSO.

DEVONS, E. and GLUCKMAN, M. (1984) 'Introduction' to GLUCKMAN, M. (Ed.), *Closed Systems and Open Minds*, Oliver and Boyd.

DOUGLAS, J.W.B. (1964) *The Home and the School*, MacGibbon and Kee.

DURKHEIM, E. (1961) *Moral Education*, Free Press.

EASTHOPE, G. (1975) *Community, Hierarchy and Open Education*, Routledge and Kegan Paul.

ESLAND, G.M. (1971) 'Teaching and learning as the organisation of knowledge', in YOUNG, M.F.D. (Ed.), *Knowledge and Control*, Macmillan.

FLETCHER, H. (1971) *Mathematics for Schools*, Addison–Wesley.

FORD, J. (1975) *Paradigms and Fairy Tales*, Routledge and Kegan Paul.

GALTON, M. and SIMON, B. (Eds) (1980) *Progress and Performance in the Primary Classroom*, Routledge and Kegan Paul.

GALTON, M., SIMON, B. and CROLL, P. (1980) *Inside the Primary Classroom*, Routledge and Kegan Paul.

GARFINKEL, H. (1967) *Studies in Ethnomethodology*, Prentice Hall.

GOFFANN, E. (1961) *Encounters*, Bobbs-Merrill.

GOODACRE, E. (1968) *Teachers and their Pupils' Home Background*, NFER.

GRANT, N. (1979) *Soviet Education*, Penguin.

GROSS, N. and TRASK, A.E. (1976) *The Sex Factor and the Management of Schools*, Wiley.

HARGREAVES, A. (1980) 'The ideology of the middle school', in HARGREAVES, A. and TICKLE, L. (Eds) *Middle Schools, Origins, Ideology and Practice*, Harper and Row.

HARGREAVES, A. (1986) *Two Cultures of Schooling: The Case of Middle Schools*, Falmer Press.

HARGREAVES, D.H. (1967) *Social Relations in a Secondary School*, Routledge and Kegan Paul.

HARGREAVES, D.H. (1978) 'Whatever happened to symbolic interactionism?', in BARTON, L., MEIGHAN, R. (Eds), *Sociological Interpretations of Schooling and Classrooms*, Nafferton.

HARTLEY, J.D. (1985) *Understanding the Primary School*, Croom Helm.

HARTLEY, J.D. (1987) 'The time of their lives. Bureaucracy in the nursery school', in POLLARD, A., (Ed), *Children and their Primary Schools*, Falmer Press.

HOWELL, A., WALKER, R. and FLETCHER, H. (1980) *Mathematics for Schools*, 2nd Edition, Addison Westley.

JACKSON, B. (1964) *Streaming: An Education System in Miniature*, Routledge and Kegan Paul.

JACKSON, P.W. (1968) *Life in Classrooms*, Holt, Rinehart and Winston.

JENCKS, C. *et al*, (1973). *Inequality*, Allen Lane.

KARABEL, J. and HALSEY, A.H. (Eds) (1977) *Power and Ideology in Education*, Oxford University Press.

KELMER-PRINGLE, M.L. *et al* (1966) *11,000 Seven Year Olds*, Longman.

KING, R.A. (1971) 'Unequal access in education — sex and social class', *Social and Economic Administration*, **3**, 3.

KING, R.A. (1973) *School Organization and Pupil Involvement*, Routledge and Kegan Paul.

KING, R.A. (1978) *All Things Bright and Beautiful? A Sociological Study of Infants' Classrooms*, Wiley.

KING, R.A. (1979) 'A search for the "invisible" pedagogy', *Sociology*, **13**, 3.

KING, R.A. (1980) 'Weberian perspectives and the study of education', *British Journal of Sociology of Education*, **1**, 1.

KING, R.A. (1980) 'Real groups and false aggregates in educational research', *Educational Studies*, **6**, 3.

KING, R.A. (1982) 'Sex composition of staff, authority and colleagiality in secondary schools', *Research in Education*, **26**.

KING, R.A. (1982) 'Organisational change in secondary schools: an action approach', *British Journal of Sociology of Education*, **3**, 1.

KING, R.A. (1983) *The Sociology of School Organisation*, Methuen.

KING, R.A. 'The man in the Wendy house: researching infants' schools', in BURGESS, R.G. (Ed.), *The Research Process in Educational Settings*, Falmer Press.

KING, R.A. (1985) 'On the "relative autonomy" of education: micro- and macro-structures', in BARTON, L. and WALKER, S. (Eds), *Education and Social Change*, Croom Helm.

KING, R.A. (1987) 'No best method: qualitative and quantitative research in the sociology of education', in WALFORD, G. (Ed.), *Doing Sociology Education*, Falmer Press.

KING, R.A. (1987) 'Sex and Social class inequalities in education: a re-examination', *British Journal of Sociology of Education*, **8**, 3.

KOUNIN, J. S. (1970) *Discipline and Group Management in Schools Classrooms*, Holt, Rinehart and Winston.

LEAT, D. (1972) 'Misunderstanding Verstehen', *Sociological Review*, **20**.

LORTIE, D.S. (1975) *School Teacher — A Sociological Analysis*, University of Chicago Press.

LYNCH, J. (1980) 'Legitimation crisis for English middle school', HARGREAVES, A. and TICKLE, L. (eds.) *Middle Schools, Origins, Ideology and Practice*, Harper and Row.

MACDOUGALL, W. (1908) *An Introduction to Social Psychology*, Methuen.

MACK, E.S. (1938) *Public Schools and British Opinion 1780–1860*, Methuen.

MORTIMORE, P., SAMMONS, P., STOLL, L., LEWIS, D. and ECOB, R. (1987) *The Junior School Project*, ILEA.

NASH, R. (1974) *Classrooms Observed*, Routledge and Kegan Paul.

NEWSON, J. and E. (1976) *Seven Year Olds in the Home Environment*, Penguin.

NORTHAM, J. (1983) 'The myth of the pre-school', *Education 3–13*, **11**, 2.

OPIE, P. and I. (1958) *The Lore and Language of Children*, Oxford University Press.

OPIE, P. and I. (1969) *Children's Games in Street and Playground*, Oxford University Press.

PARSONS, T. (1951) 'The school class as social system: some of its functions in American society', *Harvard Educational Review*, **29**.

PARSONS, T. *et al.* (1951) *The Social System*, Free Press.

POLLARD, A. (1985) *The Social World of the Primary School*, Holt.

POPPER, K.R. (1957) *The Poverty of Historicism*, Routledge and Kegan Paul.

RADICAL STATISTICS GROUP (1982) *Reading Between Numbers*, BSSRS.

RUTTER, M., MAUGHAN, B., MORTIMORE, P. OUSTON, J. (1979) *Fifteen Thousand Hours*, Open Books.

SCHUTZ, A. (1967) *Collected Papers Vol. 1. The Problem of Social Reality*, Nijhoft.

SCHUTZ, A. (1932, 1972) *The Phenomenology of the Social World*, Heinemann.

SHARP, R. and GREEN, A. with LEWIS, J. (1975) *Education and Social Control*, Routledge and Kegan Paul.

SLUCKIN, A. (1981) *Growing Up in the Playground*, Routledge.

SQUIBB, P.G. (1973) 'The concept of intelligence', *Sociological Review*, **21**.

TAYLOR, M. and GARSON, Y. (1982) *Schooling in the Middle Years*, Trentham Books.

THOMAS, W.I. (1928) *The Child in America*, Knopf.

TODD, R. and DENNISON, W.F. (1978) 'The changing role of the deputy headteacher', *Educational Review*, **30**, 3.

VAUGHAN, M. and ARCHER, M.S. (1971) *Social Conflict and Educational Change*, Cambridge University Press.

WALLACE, M. (1986) 'The rise of scale posts as a management hierarchy in schools'. *Educational Management and Administration*, **14**.

WALLER, W. (1932) *The Sociology of Teaching*, Wiley.

WEBER, M. (1948) *Essays in Sociology*, Routledge and Kegan Paul.

WEBER, M. (1964) *The Theory of Social and Economic Organisation*, Free Press.

WEBER, M. (1968) *Economy and Society*, Bedminster.

WILKINSON, A. (1966) 'English in the training of teachers', *Universities Quarterly*, **20**.

WRAGG, E. C. (1972) 'An analysis of the Verbal classroom interaction...', unpublished PhD thesis, University of Exeter.

Index